50 Premium French Bread Recipes for Home

By: Kelly Johnson

Table of Contents

- Baguette
- Pain de Campagne (French Country Bread)
- Pain Poilâne
- Pain Complet (Whole Wheat Bread)
- Pain de Mie (Square Loaf)
- Pain d'épeautre (Spelt Bread)
- Pain de Seigle (Rye Bread)
- Pain de Maïs (Cornbread)
- Pain de Noix (Nut Bread)
- Pain Viennois (Vienna Bread)
- Pain Complet aux Graines (Whole Grain Seed Bread)
- Pain au Levain (Sourdough Bread)
- Pain de Poids Chiches (Chickpea Flour Bread)
- Pain au Levain Complet (Whole Wheat Sourdough)
- Pain d'Avoine (Oat Bread)
- Pain au Lait (Milk Bread)
- Pain au Cacao (Chocolate Bread)
- Pain à l'Ancienne (Old-fashioned Bread)
- Pain de Campagne au Levain (Country Sourdough)
- Pain au Fromage (Cheese Bread)
- Pain au Romarin (Rosemary Bread)
- Pain au Beurre (Butter Bread)
- Pain au Miel (Honey Bread)
- Pain au Figues (Fig Bread)
- Pain au Cumin (Cumin Bread)
- Pain au Jambon (Ham Bread)
- Pain au Lard (Bacon Bread)
- Pain aux Olives (Olive Bread)
- Pain aux Noix et Fruits Secs (Nut and Dried Fruit Bread)
- Pain au Pesto (Pesto Bread)
- Pain à l'ail (Garlic Bread)
- Pain au Thym (Thyme Bread)

- Pain aux Herbes (Herb Bread)
- Pain au Safran (Saffron Bread)
- Pain au Citron (Lemon Bread)
- Pain aux Pommes (Apple Bread)
- Pain au Curry (Curry Bread)
- Pain au Chocolat (Chocolate-filled Bread)
- Pain au Yaourt (Yogurt Bread)
- Pain au Vin Rouge (Red Wine Bread)
- Pain de Campagne aux Épices (Spiced Country Bread)
- Pain au Poivre (Pepper Bread)
- Pain à la Moutarde (Mustard Bread)
- Pain au Chèvre (Goat Cheese Bread)
- Pain aux Framboises (Raspberry Bread)
- Pain au Basilic (Basil Bread)
- Pain au Coing (Quince Bread)
- Pain à la Pistache (Pistachio Bread)
- Pain au Cacao et Orange (Chocolate Orange Bread)
- Pain d'Échalote (Shallot Bread)

Baguette

Ingredients:

- **For the Dough:**
    - 1 1/2 cups (360 ml) lukewarm water (100°F/38°C)
    - 2 teaspoons (6 g) granulated sugar
    - 2 teaspoons (6 g) active dry yeast
    - 4 cups (500 g) all-purpose flour
    - 1 1/2 teaspoons (9 g) salt
    - 1 tablespoon (15 ml) olive oil (optional, for added tenderness)
- **For the Steam:**
    - 1 cup (240 ml) water (for creating steam in the oven)

Instructions:

1. **Prepare the Yeast Mixture:**
    - In a small bowl, combine the lukewarm water and granulated sugar. Sprinkle the active dry yeast over the top. Let it sit for about 5-10 minutes until it becomes frothy.
2. **Mix the Dough:**
    - In a large bowl, whisk together the flour and salt.
    - Make a well in the center and pour in the yeast mixture and olive oil (if using).
    - Stir with a wooden spoon or spatula until the dough begins to come together.
3. **Knead the Dough:**
    - Turn the dough out onto a lightly floured surface and knead for about 8-10 minutes until smooth and elastic. You can also use a stand mixer with a dough hook attachment to knead the dough for about 6-8 minutes.
4. **First Rise:**
    - Place the dough in a lightly oiled bowl, cover it with plastic wrap or a damp cloth, and let it rise in a warm place for about 1-1.5 hours, or until doubled in size.
5. **Shape the Baguettes:**
    - Punch down the dough and divide it into 2 or 3 equal pieces, depending on the size of the baguettes you want.
    - Shape each piece into a long, thin loaf by flattening it into a rectangle and then rolling it up tightly, pinching the seams to seal. Stretch and shape the dough into a long baguette shape, about 14-16 inches (35-40 cm) long.
    - Place the shaped baguettes on a parchment-lined baking sheet or a baguette pan. Cover with a damp cloth and let rise for another 30-45 minutes, or until slightly puffy.
6. **Preheat the Oven:**
    - Preheat your oven to 475°F (245°C). Place a small ovenproof dish filled with water on the bottom rack to create steam, which helps to develop the crispy crust.
7. **Score the Baguettes:**

- Just before baking, use a sharp knife or a razor blade to make shallow cuts (about 1/4 inch deep) along the top of each baguette. This allows the bread to expand properly during baking.
8. **Bake the Baguettes:**
    - Bake the baguettes in the preheated oven for 20-25 minutes, or until they are golden brown and have a hollow sound when tapped on the bottom.
9. **Cool:**
    - Remove the baguettes from the oven and let them cool on a wire rack.

Tips:

- **Dough Consistency:** The dough should be slightly tacky but not overly sticky. If it's too sticky, add a little more flour. If it's too dry, add a bit more water.
- **Steam:** The steam helps develop a crispy crust. You can also use a spray bottle to mist the baguettes with water before baking for added crispness.
- **Shaping:** For best results, shape the baguettes gently to avoid deflating the dough. Use a light touch when rolling and stretching.

Enjoy your homemade baguettes fresh from the oven with a pat of butter, or as the base for a delicious sandwich!

Pain de Campagne (French Country Bread)

Ingredients:

- **For the Dough:**
    - 1 1/2 cups (360 ml) warm water (110°F/45°C)
    - 2 teaspoons (6 g) granulated sugar
    - 2 teaspoons (6 g) active dry yeast
    - 1 cup (120 g) whole wheat flour
    - 2 cups (250 g) all-purpose flour
    - 1/2 cup (60 g) rye flour (optional, for added depth of flavor)
    - 1 1/2 teaspoons (9 g) salt
    - 1 tablespoon (15 ml) olive oil (optional, for added tenderness)
- **For the Starter (optional but recommended for better flavor):**
    - 1/2 cup (120 ml) water
    - 1/2 cup (60 g) all-purpose flour
    - 1/4 teaspoon (1 g) active dry yeast

Instructions:

1. **Prepare the Starter (if using):**
    - In a small bowl, mix the water, flour, and yeast. Cover with plastic wrap or a damp cloth and let it sit at room temperature for 8-12 hours, or overnight. This will develop a more complex flavor in the bread.
2. **Prepare the Yeast Mixture:**
    - In a large bowl, combine the warm water and granulated sugar. Sprinkle the active dry yeast over the top and let it sit for about 5-10 minutes until it becomes frothy.
3. **Mix the Dough:**
    - If using a starter, add it to the yeast mixture.
    - In a separate bowl, whisk together the whole wheat flour, all-purpose flour, rye flour (if using), and salt.
    - Gradually add the dry ingredients to the yeast mixture, mixing until a dough forms.
    - Stir in the olive oil if using.
4. **Knead the Dough:**
    - Turn the dough out onto a lightly floured surface and knead for about 8-10 minutes until smooth and elastic. Alternatively, use a stand mixer with a dough hook attachment to knead the dough for about 6-8 minutes.
5. **First Rise:**
    - Place the dough in a lightly oiled bowl, cover it with plastic wrap or a damp cloth, and let it rise in a warm place for about 1-1.5 hours, or until doubled in size.
6. **Shape the Dough:**
    - Punch down the dough and turn it out onto a floured surface. Shape it into a round loaf or an oval, depending on your preference.
    - Place the shaped dough on a parchment-lined baking sheet or a floured proofing basket (banneton).

7. **Second Rise:**
   - Cover the dough with a damp cloth or plastic wrap and let it rise for another 30-45 minutes, or until puffy and nearly doubled in size.
8. **Preheat the Oven:**
   - Preheat your oven to 475°F (245°C). Place a small ovenproof dish filled with water on the bottom rack to create steam, which helps develop a crispy crust.
9. **Score the Dough:**
   - Just before baking, use a sharp knife or a razor blade to make shallow cuts on the top of the dough. This allows the bread to expand properly during baking.
10. **Bake the Bread:**
    - Bake in the preheated oven for 30-35 minutes, or until the bread is golden brown and sounds hollow when tapped on the bottom.
11. **Cool:**
    - Remove the bread from the oven and let it cool on a wire rack.

Tips:

- **Texture:** Pain de Campagne has a chewy, open crumb. The combination of flours gives it a rustic texture and flavor. Adjust the flour quantities slightly if the dough feels too sticky or too dry.
- **Steam:** Creating steam in the oven helps achieve a crispy crust. If you don't have an ovenproof dish, you can mist the bread with water before baking.
- **Shaping:** For a traditional look, use a proofing basket (banneton) to shape the dough. It creates a beautiful pattern on the bread.

Enjoy your homemade Pain de Campagne with a variety of toppings, or simply with a pat of butter. It's perfect for sandwiches, soups, or just enjoying on its own!

Pain Poilâne

Ingredients:

- **For the Starter (Levain):**
  - 1/2 cup (120 ml) warm water (100°F/38°C)
  - 1/2 cup (60 g) all-purpose flour
  - 1/4 teaspoon (1 g) active dry yeast
- **For the Dough:**
  - 1 1/2 cups (360 ml) warm water (100°F/38°C)
  - 1 1/2 cups (180 g) whole wheat flour
  - 1 1/2 cups (180 g) all-purpose flour
  - 1 cup (120 g) rye flour
  - 2 teaspoons (12 g) salt
  - 1 tablespoon (15 ml) honey (optional, for a touch of sweetness)

Instructions:

1. **Prepare the Starter (Levain):**
   - In a small bowl, combine the warm water, flour, and active dry yeast. Stir well to mix.
   - Cover the bowl with plastic wrap or a damp cloth and let it sit at room temperature for about 8-12 hours, or overnight. The starter should be bubbly and slightly frothy when ready.
2. **Prepare the Dough:**
   - In a large bowl, combine the warm water and the prepared starter (levain).
   - Whisk in the whole wheat flour, all-purpose flour, rye flour, and salt. Mix until a rough dough forms. If using honey, add it now.
   - Turn the dough out onto a lightly floured surface and knead for about 8-10 minutes until smooth and elastic. The dough should be somewhat sticky but manageable. You can also use a stand mixer with a dough hook attachment for this step.
3. **First Rise:**
   - Place the dough in a lightly oiled bowl, cover it with plastic wrap or a damp cloth, and let it rise in a warm place for about 1-1.5 hours, or until doubled in size.
4. **Shape the Dough:**
   - Punch down the dough to release air bubbles. Turn it out onto a floured surface and shape it into a round loaf.
   - Place the shaped dough onto a parchment-lined baking sheet or into a lightly floured proofing basket (banneton).
5. **Second Rise:**
   - Cover the dough with a damp cloth or plastic wrap and let it rise for another 30-45 minutes, or until it has puffed up noticeably.
6. **Preheat the Oven:**
   - Preheat your oven to 475°F (245°C). Place a small ovenproof dish filled with water on the bottom rack to create steam, which helps develop a crispy crust.
7. **Score the Dough:**
   - Just before baking, use a sharp knife or a razor blade to make shallow cuts on the top of the dough. This allows the bread to expand properly during baking.
8. **Bake the Bread:**
   - Bake in the preheated oven for 35-45 minutes, or until the bread is deeply golden brown and sounds hollow when tapped on the bottom.
9. **Cool:**
   - Remove the bread from the oven and let it cool on a wire rack.

Tips:

- **Dough Consistency:** The dough for Pain Poilâne should be slightly sticky. If it's too sticky, add a bit more flour. If too dry, add a bit more water.
- **Steam:** The steam helps create a crispy crust, so don't skip the steam step. You can also mist the bread with water before baking for additional crispness.

- **Shaping:** For a classic look, use a round proofing basket (banneton) to shape the dough. This will give the bread a traditional appearance.

Enjoy your Pain Poilâne fresh with a pat of butter, or use it for sandwiches and toasts. Its complex flavor and hearty texture make it a versatile and delicious choice for any meal!

Pain Complet (Whole Wheat Bread)

Ingredients:

- **For the Dough:**
    - 1 1/2 cups (360 ml) warm water (110°F/45°C)
    - 2 teaspoons (6 g) granulated sugar
    - 2 teaspoons (6 g) active dry yeast
    - 3 1/2 cups (440 g) whole wheat flour
    - 1 cup (120 g) all-purpose flour (optional, for a lighter texture)
    - 1 1/2 teaspoons (9 g) salt
    - 2 tablespoons (30 ml) olive oil (optional, for added softness)

Instructions:

1. **Prepare the Yeast Mixture:**
    - In a small bowl, combine the warm water and granulated sugar. Sprinkle the active dry yeast over the top. Let it sit for about 5-10 minutes until it becomes frothy and bubbles up.
2. **Mix the Dough:**
    - In a large mixing bowl, whisk together the whole wheat flour and all-purpose flour (if using), and salt.
    - Make a well in the center of the dry ingredients and pour in the yeast mixture and olive oil (if using).
    - Stir with a wooden spoon or spatula until the dough begins to come together.
3. **Knead the Dough:**
    - Turn the dough out onto a lightly floured surface. Knead for about 8-10 minutes until smooth and elastic. The dough should be slightly sticky but manageable. You can also use a stand mixer with a dough hook attachment for this step, kneading for about 6-8 minutes.
4. **First Rise:**
    - Place the dough in a lightly oiled bowl, cover it with plastic wrap or a damp cloth, and let it rise in a warm place for about 1-1.5 hours, or until doubled in size.
5. **Shape the Dough:**
    - Punch down the dough to release air bubbles. Turn it out onto a floured surface and shape it into a loaf. You can shape it into a traditional loaf or into smaller individual loaves if preferred.
    - Place the shaped dough into a lightly greased loaf pan or onto a parchment-lined baking sheet.

6. **Second Rise:**
   - Cover the dough with a damp cloth or plastic wrap and let it rise for another 30-45 minutes, or until puffy and nearly doubled in size.
7. **Preheat the Oven:**
   - Preheat your oven to 375°F (190°C).
8. **Bake the Bread:**
   - Bake the bread in the preheated oven for 30-40 minutes, or until the loaf is golden brown and sounds hollow when tapped on the bottom.
9. **Cool:**
   - Remove the bread from the oven and let it cool on a wire rack before slicing.

Tips:

- **Dough Consistency:** Whole wheat dough tends to be a bit denser than white bread dough. If the dough feels too dry, add a bit more water. If it's too sticky, add a little more flour.
- **Texture:** For a lighter texture, you can substitute part of the whole wheat flour with all-purpose flour. This also helps in achieving a better rise.
- **Flavor Additions:** Consider adding seeds like sunflower or sesame, or nuts and dried fruits to the dough for added texture and flavor.

Enjoy your Pain Complet fresh from the oven, or toasted with a bit of butter and your favorite spreads. Its hearty flavor and nutritional benefits make it a perfect choice for everyday baking!

Pain de Mie (Square Loaf)

Ingredients:

- **For the Dough:**
    - 1 cup (240 ml) warm milk (110°F/45°C)
    - 1/4 cup (50 g) granulated sugar
    - 2 1/4 teaspoons (7 g) active dry yeast (or instant yeast)
    - 3 cups (375 g) all-purpose flour
    - 1 cup (120 g) bread flour (optional, for a lighter texture)
    - 1 1/2 teaspoons (9 g) salt
    - 1/4 cup (60 g) unsalted butter, softened
    - 1 large egg
- **For the Pan:**
    - 1 Pain de Mie pan with a lid (also called a Pullman pan)

Instructions:

1. **Prepare the Yeast Mixture:**
   - In a small bowl, combine the warm milk and granulated sugar. Sprinkle the active dry yeast over the top and let it sit for about 5-10 minutes, until it becomes frothy.

If you are using instant yeast, you can skip this step and add the yeast directly to the flour.
2. **Mix the Dough:**
    - In a large bowl, whisk together the all-purpose flour, bread flour (if using), and salt.
    - Make a well in the center of the dry ingredients. Add the yeast mixture, softened butter, and egg.
    - Stir with a wooden spoon or spatula until the dough begins to come together.
3. **Knead the Dough:**
    - Turn the dough out onto a lightly floured surface and knead for about 8-10 minutes, until smooth and elastic. You can also use a stand mixer with a dough hook attachment to knead the dough for about 6-8 minutes.
4. **First Rise:**
    - Place the dough in a lightly oiled bowl, cover it with plastic wrap or a damp cloth, and let it rise in a warm place for about 1-1.5 hours, or until doubled in size.
5. **Shape the Dough:**
    - Punch down the dough to release air bubbles. Turn it out onto a floured surface and shape it into a rectangle that fits the size of your Pain de Mie pan.
    - Place the shaped dough into the greased Pain de Mie pan.
6. **Second Rise:**
    - Cover the pan with the lid or plastic wrap and let it rise for another 30-45 minutes, or until the dough has risen just below the lid.
7. **Preheat the Oven:**
    - Preheat your oven to 375°F (190°C).
8. **Bake the Bread:**
    - Place the Pain de Mie pan in the preheated oven. Bake for 30-40 minutes, or until the bread is golden brown and sounds hollow when tapped on the bottom.
    - If using the lid, you can remove it during the last 10 minutes of baking to allow the top to brown.
9. **Cool:**
    - Remove the bread from the oven and let it cool in the pan for about 10 minutes. Then, remove the bread from the pan and let it cool completely on a wire rack before slicing.

Tips:

- **Dough Consistency:** The dough should be soft and slightly tacky but not sticky. Adjust the flour or milk as needed to achieve the right consistency.
- **Pan Preparation:** Grease the Pain de Mie pan well to ensure the bread comes out easily. You can also line it with parchment paper.
- **Texture:** For a finer crumb, you can use bread flour in place of some of the all-purpose flour.

Pain de Mie is perfect for sandwiches or as a base for French toast. Its even texture and soft crumb make it a versatile and delightful addition to your baking repertoire. Enjoy!

Pain d'épeautre (Spelt Bread)

Ingredients:

- **For the Dough:**
    - 1 1/2 cups (360 ml) warm water (110°F/45°C)
    - 2 teaspoons (6 g) granulated sugar or honey
    - 2 teaspoons (6 g) active dry yeast (or instant yeast)
    - 3 1/2 cups (440 g) spelt flour
    - 1 cup (120 g) all-purpose flour (optional, for a lighter texture)
    - 1 1/2 teaspoons (9 g) salt
    - 1/4 cup (60 ml) olive oil (optional, for added softness)

Instructions:

1. **Prepare the Yeast Mixture:**
    - In a small bowl, combine the warm water and sugar or honey. Sprinkle the yeast over the top and let it sit for about 5-10 minutes until it becomes frothy. If using instant yeast, you can skip this step and add it directly to the flour.
2. **Mix the Dough:**
    - In a large bowl, whisk together the spelt flour and all-purpose flour (if using), and salt.
    - Make a well in the center of the dry ingredients. Add the yeast mixture and olive oil (if using).
    - Stir with a wooden spoon or spatula until the dough starts to come together.
3. **Knead the Dough:**
    - Turn the dough out onto a lightly floured surface and knead for about 8-10 minutes until smooth and elastic. The dough should be slightly sticky but manageable. You can also use a stand mixer with a dough hook attachment for this step, kneading for about 6-8 minutes.
4. **First Rise:**
    - Place the dough in a lightly oiled bowl, cover it with plastic wrap or a damp cloth, and let it rise in a warm place for about 1-1.5 hours, or until doubled in size.
5. **Shape the Dough:**
    - Punch down the dough to release air bubbles. Turn it out onto a floured surface and shape it into a loaf.
    - Place the shaped dough into a lightly greased loaf pan or onto a parchment-lined baking sheet.
6. **Second Rise:**
    - Cover the dough with a damp cloth or plastic wrap and let it rise for another 30-45 minutes, or until puffy and nearly doubled in size.
7. **Preheat the Oven:**

- Preheat your oven to 375°F (190°C).
8. **Bake the Bread:**
    - Bake in the preheated oven for 30-40 minutes, or until the bread is golden brown and sounds hollow when tapped on the bottom.
9. **Cool:**
    - Remove the bread from the oven and let it cool on a wire rack before slicing.

Tips:

- **Texture:** Spelt flour can vary in its moisture absorption, so adjust the amount of flour or water as needed. The dough should be soft and slightly sticky but workable.
- **Flavor Additions:** You can add seeds (such as sunflower or sesame), nuts, or dried fruits to the dough for extra flavor and texture.
- **Pan Preparation:** Ensure your loaf pan is well-greased or lined with parchment paper to prevent sticking.

Pain d'épeautre is a wonderful bread with a unique flavor profile. It's excellent for sandwiches, toasted with a bit of butter, or as a base for your favorite spreads. Enjoy baking and tasting this nutritious and flavorful bread!

Pain de Seigle (Rye Bread)

Ingredients:

- **For the Dough:**
    - 1 1/2 cups (360 ml) warm water (110°F/45°C)
    - 2 teaspoons (6 g) granulated sugar
    - 2 teaspoons (6 g) active dry yeast (or instant yeast)
    - 2 cups (240 g) rye flour
    - 1 1/2 cups (180 g) all-purpose flour (optional, for a lighter texture)
    - 1 1/2 teaspoons (9 g) salt
    - 2 tablespoons (30 ml) caraway seeds (optional, for traditional flavor)
    - 2 tablespoons (30 ml) vegetable oil (optional, for added softness)

Instructions:

1. **Prepare the Yeast Mixture:**
    - In a small bowl, combine the warm water and granulated sugar. Sprinkle the yeast over the top and let it sit for about 5-10 minutes, until it becomes frothy. If you are using instant yeast, you can skip this step and add the yeast directly to the flour.
2. **Mix the Dough:**
    - In a large bowl, whisk together the rye flour, all-purpose flour (if using), salt, and caraway seeds (if using).

- Make a well in the center of the dry ingredients. Add the yeast mixture and vegetable oil (if using).
- Stir with a wooden spoon or spatula until the dough starts to come together.
3. **Knead the Dough:**
   - Turn the dough out onto a lightly floured surface. Knead for about 8-10 minutes, or until the dough is smooth and elastic. Rye dough will be stickier than wheat dough, so you may need to add a bit more flour if it's too sticky.
   - You can also use a stand mixer with a dough hook attachment to knead the dough for about 6-8 minutes.
4. **First Rise:**
   - Place the dough in a lightly oiled bowl, cover it with plastic wrap or a damp cloth, and let it rise in a warm place for about 1-1.5 hours, or until doubled in size.
5. **Shape the Dough:**
   - Punch down the dough to release air bubbles. Turn it out onto a floured surface and shape it into a loaf.
   - Place the shaped dough into a lightly greased loaf pan or onto a parchment-lined baking sheet.
6. **Second Rise:**
   - Cover the dough with a damp cloth or plastic wrap and let it rise for another 30-45 minutes, or until puffy and nearly doubled in size.
7. **Preheat the Oven:**
   - Preheat your oven to 375°F (190°C).
8. **Bake the Bread:**
   - Bake in the preheated oven for 30-40 minutes, or until the bread is deeply golden brown and sounds hollow when tapped on the bottom.
9. **Cool:**
   - Remove the bread from the oven and let it cool on a wire rack before slicing.

Tips:

- **Dough Consistency:** Rye dough is often denser and stickier than wheat dough. Adjust the flour or water to achieve a workable consistency. The dough should be soft and slightly tacky.
- **Caraway Seeds:** Traditional rye bread often includes caraway seeds for additional flavor. You can adjust the amount to your taste or omit them if you prefer a milder bread.
- **Texture:** For a lighter rye bread, you can substitute a portion of the rye flour with all-purpose flour. If you prefer a denser bread, use more rye flour.

Pain de Seigle is perfect for sandwiches, particularly with hearty fillings like pastrami or smoked salmon, or simply enjoyed with a spread of butter. Its robust flavor and dense texture make it a satisfying and versatile bread. Enjoy your baking!

Pain de Maïs (Cornbread)

Ingredients:

- **For the Cornbread:**
    - 1 cup (120 g) cornmeal
    - 1 cup (120 g) all-purpose flour
    - 1/4 cup (50 g) granulated sugar (adjust to taste)
    - 1 tablespoon (15 g) baking powder
    - 1/2 teaspoon (3 g) salt
    - 1 cup (240 ml) milk
    - 1/4 cup (60 ml) vegetable oil or melted butter
    - 2 large eggs
- **Optional Add-ins:**
    - 1 cup (150 g) corn kernels (fresh, frozen, or canned, drained)
    - 1/2 cup (60 g) shredded cheese (cheddar or your choice)
    - 1/4 cup (60 ml) chopped jalapeños or green chilies
    - 1/4 cup (60 ml) chopped fresh herbs (such as chives or parsley)

Instructions:

1. **Preheat the Oven:**
    - Preheat your oven to 400°F (200°C). Grease an 8-inch (20 cm) square baking pan or a similarly sized ovenproof dish.
2. **Mix Dry Ingredients:**
    - In a large bowl, whisk together the cornmeal, all-purpose flour, granulated sugar, baking powder, and salt.
3. **Mix Wet Ingredients:**
    - In another bowl, whisk together the milk, vegetable oil (or melted butter), and eggs.
4. **Combine Ingredients:**
    - Pour the wet ingredients into the dry ingredients. Stir until just combined; the batter will be lumpy. Be careful not to overmix.
5. **Add Optional Ingredients:**
    - If using, fold in corn kernels, shredded cheese, chopped jalapeños, or herbs.
6. **Pour and Bake:**
    - Pour the batter into the greased baking pan and spread it out evenly.
7. **Bake:**
    - Bake in the preheated oven for 20-25 minutes, or until the cornbread is golden brown and a toothpick inserted into the center comes out clean.
8. **Cool:**
    - Allow the cornbread to cool in the pan for about 10 minutes before cutting into squares or wedges. Serve warm or at room temperature.

Tips:

- **Texture:** For a slightly denser cornbread, use more cornmeal and less flour. For a lighter texture, increase the amount of flour relative to the cornmeal.
- **Sweetness:** Adjust the amount of sugar based on your preference. Some prefer cornbread less sweet, while others enjoy a touch of sweetness.
- **Variations:** Experiment with add-ins like cooked bacon, diced onions, or other types of cheese to customize the flavor of your cornbread.

Pain de Maïs is versatile and can be served with a variety of dishes. It's perfect for a comforting side with chili or as a standalone treat with a pat of butter. Enjoy your homemade cornbread!

Pain de Noix (Nut Bread)

Ingredients:

- **For the Dough:**
    - 1 1/2 cups (360 ml) warm water (110°F/45°C)
    - 2 teaspoons (6 g) granulated sugar
    - 2 teaspoons (6 g) active dry yeast (or instant yeast)
    - 3 1/2 cups (440 g) all-purpose flour
    - 1 1/2 teaspoons (9 g) salt
    - 1/4 cup (60 ml) olive oil or melted butter
    - 1 cup (120 g) mixed nuts (such as walnuts, pecans, and hazelnuts), roughly chopped
- **Optional:**
    - 1/2 cup (60 g) dried fruit (such as raisins or cranberries), for added sweetness
    - 1 tablespoon (15 g) honey or maple syrup, for a touch of sweetness

Instructions:

1. **Prepare the Yeast Mixture:**
    - In a small bowl, combine the warm water and granulated sugar. Sprinkle the yeast over the top and let it sit for about 5-10 minutes until it becomes frothy. If you are using instant yeast, you can skip this step and add it directly to the flour.
2. **Mix the Dough:**
    - In a large bowl, whisk together the all-purpose flour and salt.
    - Make a well in the center of the dry ingredients. Add the yeast mixture and olive oil (or melted butter).
    - Stir with a wooden spoon or spatula until the dough starts to come together.
3. **Add Nuts and Optional Ingredients:**
    - Once the dough starts to come together, fold in the chopped nuts and dried fruit (if using). Mix until the nuts and fruit are evenly distributed throughout the dough.
4. **Knead the Dough:**
    - Turn the dough out onto a lightly floured surface and knead for about 8-10 minutes, or until smooth and elastic. You can also use a stand mixer with a dough hook attachment to knead the dough for about 6-8 minutes.
5. **First Rise:**
    - Place the dough in a lightly oiled bowl, cover it with plastic wrap or a damp cloth, and let it rise in a warm place for about 1-1.5 hours, or until doubled in size.
6. **Shape the Dough:**
    - Punch down the dough to release air bubbles. Turn it out onto a floured surface and shape it into a loaf or divide it into smaller pieces for rolls.
    - Place the shaped dough into a greased loaf pan or onto a parchment-lined baking sheet.
7. **Second Rise:**
    - Cover the dough with a damp cloth or plastic wrap and let it rise for another 30-45 minutes, or until puffy and nearly doubled in size.
8. **Preheat the Oven:**

- Preheat your oven to 375°F (190°C).
9. **Bake the Bread:**
    - Bake in the preheated oven for 30-40 minutes, or until the bread is golden brown and sounds hollow when tapped on the bottom.
10. **Cool:**
    - Remove the bread from the oven and let it cool in the pan for about 10 minutes before transferring it to a wire rack to cool completely.

Tips:

- **Nuts:** Feel free to use your favorite nuts or a combination of different kinds. Toasting the nuts slightly before adding them to the dough can enhance their flavor.
- **Sweetness:** If you prefer a sweeter bread, you can add a bit of honey or maple syrup to the dough.
- **Texture:** For a more rustic loaf, you can leave the dough a bit rough and uneven, or shape it into a round loaf for a different presentation.

Pain de Noix is a versatile bread that pairs well with a variety of toppings and is perfect for snacking or as part of a meal. Enjoy the rich, nutty flavor of this delightful bread!

Pain Viennois (Vienna Bread)

Ingredients:

- **For the Dough:**
    - 1 cup (240 ml) warm milk (110°F/45°C)
    - 2 teaspoons (6 g) granulated sugar
    - 2 teaspoons (6 g) active dry yeast (or instant yeast)
    - 3 1/2 cups (440 g) all-purpose flour
    - 1/2 teaspoon (3 g) salt
    - 1/4 cup (50 g) granulated sugar (for dough)
    - 1/2 cup (115 g) unsalted butter, softened
    - 2 large eggs
- **For the Egg Wash:**
    - 1 large egg, beaten
    - 1 tablespoon (15 ml) milk

Instructions:

1. **Prepare the Yeast Mixture:**
    - In a small bowl, combine the warm milk and 2 teaspoons of granulated sugar. Sprinkle the yeast over the top and let it sit for about 5-10 minutes, until it becomes frothy. If using instant yeast, you can skip this step and add it directly to the flour.
2. **Mix the Dough:**
    - In a large bowl, whisk together the flour, 1/2 teaspoon salt, and 1/4 cup granulated sugar.
    - Make a well in the center of the dry ingredients. Add the yeast mixture, softened butter, and eggs.
    - Stir with a wooden spoon or spatula until the dough starts to come together.
3. **Knead the Dough:**
    - Turn the dough out onto a lightly floured surface and knead for about 8-10 minutes, or until smooth and elastic. You can also use a stand mixer with a dough hook attachment to knead the dough for about 6-8 minutes.
4. **First Rise:**
    - Place the dough in a lightly oiled bowl, cover it with plastic wrap or a damp cloth, and let it rise in a warm place for about 1-1.5 hours, or until doubled in size.
5. **Shape the Dough:**
    - Punch down the dough to release air bubbles. Turn it out onto a floured surface and shape it into a loaf or divide it into smaller pieces for rolls.
    - Place the shaped dough into a greased loaf pan or onto a parchment-lined baking sheet.
6. **Second Rise:**
    - Cover the dough with a damp cloth or plastic wrap and let it rise for another 30-45 minutes, or until puffy and nearly doubled in size.
7. **Preheat the Oven:**
    - Preheat your oven to 375°F (190°C).

8. **Prepare the Egg Wash:**
    - In a small bowl, mix the beaten egg with 1 tablespoon of milk. Brush the egg wash over the top of the dough to give it a golden, shiny finish.
9. **Bake the Bread:**
    - Bake in the preheated oven for 25-35 minutes, or until the bread is golden brown and sounds hollow when tapped on the bottom.
10. **Cool:**
    - Remove the bread from the oven and let it cool on a wire rack before slicing.

Tips:

- **Butter:** Ensure the butter is softened but not melted, as it helps in achieving a light and tender crumb.
- **Flavor Variations:** You can add a touch of vanilla extract to the dough for a hint of sweetness or sprinkle a bit of cinnamon and sugar on top before baking for a sweet crust.
- **Texture:** For a softer crust, cover the bread with aluminum foil for the last 10 minutes of baking.

Pain Viennois is a delightful bread that's perfect for breakfast, brunch, or as a base for sandwiches. Its soft texture and subtle sweetness make it versatile and enjoyable on its own or with various spreads. Enjoy your baking!

Pain Complet aux Graines (Whole Grain Seed Bread)

Ingredients:

- **For the Dough:**
    - 1 1/2 cups (360 ml) warm water (110°F/45°C)
    - 2 teaspoons (6 g) granulated sugar
    - 2 teaspoons (6 g) active dry yeast (or instant yeast)
    - 2 cups (240 g) whole wheat flour
    - 1 cup (120 g) all-purpose flour
    - 1/4 cup (30 g) sunflower seeds
    - 1/4 cup (30 g) flaxseeds
    - 1/4 cup (30 g) sesame seeds
    - 1/4 cup (30 g) pumpkin seeds
    - 1 1/2 teaspoons (9 g) salt
    - 2 tablespoons (30 ml) olive oil

Instructions:

1. **Prepare the Yeast Mixture:**

- In a small bowl, combine the warm water and granulated sugar. Sprinkle the yeast over the top and let it sit for about 5-10 minutes until it becomes frothy. If using instant yeast, you can skip this step and add it directly to the flour.

2. **Mix the Dough:**
   - In a large bowl, whisk together the whole wheat flour, all-purpose flour, salt, and a mix of seeds (reserving a small amount of seeds for topping if desired).
   - Make a well in the center of the dry ingredients. Add the yeast mixture and olive oil.
   - Stir with a wooden spoon or spatula until the dough begins to come together.
3. **Knead the Dough:**
   - Turn the dough out onto a lightly floured surface and knead for about 8-10 minutes, or until the dough is smooth and elastic. You can also use a stand mixer with a dough hook attachment to knead the dough for about 6-8 minutes.
4. **First Rise:**
   - Place the dough in a lightly oiled bowl, cover it with plastic wrap or a damp cloth, and let it rise in a warm place for about 1-1.5 hours, or until doubled in size.
5. **Shape the Dough:**
   - Punch down the dough to release air bubbles. Turn it out onto a floured surface and shape it into a loaf or divide it into smaller pieces if you prefer rolls.
   - Place the shaped dough into a greased loaf pan or onto a parchment-lined baking sheet. If desired, sprinkle the top with additional seeds.
6. **Second Rise:**
   - Cover the dough with a damp cloth or plastic wrap and let it rise for another 30-45 minutes, or until puffy and nearly doubled in size.
7. **Preheat the Oven:**
   - Preheat your oven to 375°F (190°C).
8. **Bake the Bread:**
   - Bake in the preheated oven for 30-40 minutes, or until the bread is golden brown and sounds hollow when tapped on the bottom.
9. **Cool:**
   - Remove the bread from the oven and let it cool on a wire rack before slicing.

Tips:

- **Seed Mixture:** Feel free to adjust the types and proportions of seeds to your preference. You can also add other seeds like chia or hemp seeds.
- **Texture:** For a softer crust, you can cover the bread with aluminum foil for the last 10 minutes of baking.
- **Flavor Variations:** Add a tablespoon of honey or molasses to the dough for a touch of sweetness or mix in some dried herbs for extra flavor.

Pain Complet aux Graines is a nutritious and flavorful bread that's perfect for sandwiches, toast, or served with a hearty soup. Enjoy the wholesome taste and the satisfying crunch of the seeds!

Pain au Levain (Sourdough Bread)

Ingredients:

For the Starter:

- 50 grams all-purpose flour
- 50 grams water
- 1 tablespoon sourdough starter (if you don't have one, you can create a starter over a week or so by mixing flour and water and letting it ferment)

For the Dough:

- 500 grams all-purpose flour or bread flour
- 350 grams water (room temperature)
- 100 grams active sourdough starter (at 100% hydration, meaning equal parts flour and water by weight)
- 10 grams salt

Instructions:

1. Prepare the Starter:

- **Feed Your Starter:** If your starter is in the fridge, take it out 12-24 hours before you start your dough to get it active. Feed it with equal parts flour and water, and let it sit at room temperature.

2. Mix the Dough:

- **Autolyse:** In a large bowl, combine the flour and water. Mix until there are no dry spots. Cover the bowl and let it rest for 30 minutes to an hour. This process helps with the dough's extensibility.
- **Add Starter and Salt:** Add the sourdough starter and salt to the dough. Mix until fully incorporated. The dough will be sticky and shaggy at this point.

3. Knead the Dough:

- **Initial Knead:** On a lightly floured surface, knead the dough for about 10 minutes. Alternatively, you can use the stretch and fold method in the bowl. To do this, stretch the dough and fold it over itself every 30 minutes for 2 hours. This helps develop gluten without overworking the dough.

4. Bulk Fermentation:

- **First Rise:** Transfer the dough to a lightly oiled bowl, cover it with a damp cloth or plastic wrap, and let it rise at room temperature for about 4-6 hours, or until it has doubled in size. The time can vary depending on the ambient temperature and the strength of your starter.

5. Shape the Dough:

- **Pre-Shaping:** Turn the dough out onto a lightly floured surface. Gently shape it into a round or oval shape, cover it, and let it rest for 20-30 minutes.
- **Final Shaping:** Shape the dough into your desired shape (round or oval) and place it in a well-floured proofing basket or bowl. Cover it again and let it rise for another 2-3 hours, or until it has visibly expanded.

6. Preheat the Oven:

- **Heat Up:** About 30 minutes before baking, preheat your oven to 450°F (230°C). If you have a Dutch oven or a baking cloche, place it in the oven to preheat as well.

7. Bake the Bread:

- **Score the Dough:** Carefully transfer the dough onto a piece of parchment paper. Using a sharp blade or a bread lame, score the top of the dough to allow it to expand properly.
- **Bake:** If using a Dutch oven, place the dough (with the parchment paper) into the preheated Dutch oven, cover with the lid, and bake for 20 minutes. After 20 minutes, remove the lid and bake for an additional 20-25 minutes, or until the crust is deep brown and the bread sounds hollow when tapped on the bottom.
- **Without a Dutch Oven:** Place the dough directly on a preheated baking stone or a baking sheet. Bake for 35-40 minutes, or until the crust is golden and the bread sounds hollow when tapped.

8. Cool the Bread:

- **Rest:** Let the bread cool completely on a wire rack before slicing. This allows the interior to set and develop flavor.

Enjoy your homemade Pain au Levain!

Pain de Poids Chiches (Chickpea Flour Bread)

Ingredients:

- 200 grams chickpea flour (also known as gram flour or besan)
- 200 grams all-purpose flour (or gluten-free flour blend if you prefer)
- 300 grams water (room temperature)
- 2 tablespoons olive oil
- 1 tablespoon honey (or sugar, if preferred)
- 1 teaspoon salt
- 1 teaspoon baking powder

- 1/2 teaspoon baking soda
- 1 tablespoon ground flaxseeds (optional, for added texture)
- 1/2 teaspoon ground cumin or coriander (optional, for extra flavor)

Instructions:

1. Prepare the Oven:

- Preheat your oven to 375°F (190°C). Grease a loaf pan or line it with parchment paper.

2. Mix the Dry Ingredients:

- In a large bowl, whisk together the chickpea flour, all-purpose flour, baking powder, baking soda, salt, and optional spices (cumin or coriander). If you're using ground flaxseeds, add them here as well.

3. Combine Wet Ingredients:

- In a separate bowl, mix the water, olive oil, and honey (or sugar) until well combined.

4. Combine Wet and Dry Ingredients:

- Pour the wet mixture into the dry ingredients. Stir until just combined. The batter will be somewhat thick but should be pourable.

5. Transfer to Pan:

- Pour the batter into the prepared loaf pan and smooth the top with a spatula.

6. Bake the Bread:

- Bake in the preheated oven for 40-45 minutes, or until the top is golden brown and a toothpick inserted into the center comes out clean.

7. Cool the Bread:

- Allow the bread to cool in the pan for about 10 minutes, then transfer it to a wire rack to cool completely before slicing.

This bread is delicious on its own or with a variety of spreads, cheeses, or as a base for savory toppings. Enjoy your homemade Pain de Poids Chiches!

Pain au Levain Complet (Whole Wheat Sourdough)

Ingredients:

For the Starter:

- 50 grams whole wheat flour
- 50 grams water
- 1 tablespoon active sourdough starter (if you don't have a starter, you'll need to create or acquire one in advance)

For the Dough:

- 400 grams whole wheat flour
- 100 grams all-purpose flour (optional, for a lighter texture)
- 350 grams water (room temperature)
- 100 grams active sourdough starter (at 100% hydration, meaning equal parts flour and water by weight)
- 10 grams salt

Instructions:

1. Prepare the Starter:

- **Feed Your Starter:** If your starter is in the fridge, take it out 12-24 hours before you start your dough to get it active. Feed it with equal parts whole wheat flour and water, and let it sit at room temperature.

2. Mix the Dough:

- **Autolyse:** In a large bowl, combine the whole wheat flour (and all-purpose flour, if using) with 350 grams of water. Mix until there are no dry spots. Cover the bowl and let it rest for 30 minutes to an hour. This helps with gluten development and improves the dough's texture.
- **Add Starter and Salt:** Add the sourdough starter and salt to the dough. Mix until fully incorporated. The dough will be sticky and shaggy at this stage.

3. Knead the Dough:

- **Initial Knead:** On a lightly floured surface, knead the dough for about 10 minutes. Alternatively, you can use the stretch and fold method. Stretch the dough and fold it over itself every 30 minutes for 2 hours. This method helps develop gluten without overworking the dough.

4. Bulk Fermentation:

- **First Rise:** Transfer the dough to a lightly oiled bowl, cover it with a damp cloth or plastic wrap, and let it rise at room temperature for about 4-6 hours, or until it has doubled in size. The timing can vary based on your room temperature and the strength of your starter.

5. Shape the Dough:

- **Pre-Shaping:** Turn the dough out onto a lightly floured surface. Gently shape it into a round or oval shape, cover it, and let it rest for 20-30 minutes.
- **Final Shaping:** Shape the dough into your desired shape and place it in a well-floured proofing basket or bowl. Cover it again and let it rise for another 2-3 hours, or until it has visibly expanded.

6. Preheat the Oven:

- **Heat Up:** About 30 minutes before baking, preheat your oven to 450°F (230°C). If you have a Dutch oven or a baking cloche, place it in the oven to preheat as well.

7. Bake the Bread:

- **Score the Dough:** Carefully transfer the dough onto a piece of parchment paper. Use a sharp blade or a bread lame to score the top of the dough. Scoring allows the bread to expand properly.
- **Bake:** If using a Dutch oven, place the dough (with the parchment paper) into the preheated Dutch oven, cover with the lid, and bake for 20 minutes. After 20 minutes, remove the lid and bake for an additional 20-25 minutes, or until the crust is deep brown and the bread sounds hollow when tapped on the bottom.
- **Without a Dutch Oven:** Place the dough directly on a preheated baking stone or a baking sheet. Bake for 35-40 minutes, or until the crust is golden and the bread sounds hollow when tapped.

8. Cool the Bread:

- **Rest:** Let the bread cool completely on a wire rack before slicing. This allows the interior to set and develop its full flavor.

Enjoy your whole wheat sourdough bread! It's perfect for sandwiches, toasting, or just enjoying with a bit of butter.

Pain d'Avoine (Oat Bread)

Ingredients:

For the Dough:

- 200 grams rolled oats (not instant)
- 300 grams all-purpose flour or bread flour
- 200 grams whole wheat flour
- 350 grams water (room temperature)
- 100 grams active sourdough starter (optional, for added flavor and texture)
- 2 tablespoons honey or maple syrup
- 2 tablespoons olive oil or melted butter
- 1 tablespoon salt

- 1 tablespoon active dry yeast (if not using sourdough starter)

Instructions:

1. Prepare the Oats:

- **Soak the Oats:** Place the rolled oats in a bowl and cover them with 350 grams of water. Let them soak for at least 30 minutes to soften.

2. Prepare the Dough:

- **Mix Dry Ingredients:** In a large mixing bowl, whisk together the all-purpose flour (or bread flour), whole wheat flour, and salt.
- **Activate Yeast (if not using sourdough starter):** In a small bowl, dissolve the active dry yeast in a bit of warm water (about 100°F or 38°C) and let it sit for 5-10 minutes until frothy.
- **Combine Ingredients:** If using a sourdough starter, add it directly to the soaked oats. If using yeast, add it to the oats along with the honey or maple syrup and olive oil. Mix well.
- **Add Wet Ingredients:** Pour the soaked oats and yeast mixture into the dry ingredients. Mix until well combined. The dough will be slightly sticky.

3. Knead the Dough:

- **Knead:** Turn the dough onto a lightly floured surface and knead for about 8-10 minutes, or until the dough is smooth and elastic. If the dough is too sticky, add a bit more flour as needed.

4. Bulk Fermentation:

- **First Rise:** Place the dough in a lightly oiled bowl, cover with a damp cloth or plastic wrap, and let it rise at room temperature for about 1-2 hours, or until it has doubled in size.

5. Shape the Dough:

- **Pre-Shape:** Turn the dough out onto a lightly floured surface. Gently shape it into a round or oval loaf.
- **Final Shaping:** Place the shaped dough into a greased loaf pan or on a baking sheet. Cover it and let it rise for another 30-60 minutes, or until it has risen noticeably.

6. Preheat the Oven:

- Preheat your oven to 375°F (190°C).

7. Bake the Bread:

- **Bake:** Place the loaf in the preheated oven and bake for 35-40 minutes, or until the bread is golden brown and sounds hollow when tapped on the bottom.

8. Cool the Bread:

- **Rest:** Remove the bread from the oven and let it cool in the pan for 10 minutes before transferring it to a wire rack to cool completely.

This oat bread is perfect for a wholesome breakfast or as a sandwich base. Enjoy its hearty texture and slightly sweet flavor!

Pain au Lait (Milk Bread)

Ingredients:

- 500 grams all-purpose flour
- 250 ml whole milk (warm)
- 50 grams sugar
- 10 grams salt
- 10 grams active dry yeast (or 15 grams fresh yeast)
- 60 grams unsalted butter (softened)
- 1 large egg
- 1 teaspoon vanilla extract (optional)

Instructions:

1. Prepare the Yeast:

- **Activate Yeast:** If using active dry yeast, dissolve it in the warm milk with a pinch of sugar and let it sit for 5-10 minutes until it becomes frothy. If using fresh yeast, crumble it into the milk and let it dissolve for a few minutes.

2. Mix the Dough:

- **Combine Dry Ingredients:** In a large mixing bowl, whisk together the flour, sugar, and salt.
- **Add Wet Ingredients:** Make a well in the center of the dry ingredients and add the activated yeast mixture, egg, and vanilla extract (if using). Mix until the dough starts to come together.
- **Incorporate Butter:** Add the softened butter to the dough. Knead the dough on a lightly floured surface for about 10 minutes, or until it is smooth and elastic.

3. First Rise:

- **Bulk Fermentation:** Place the dough in a lightly oiled bowl, cover it with a damp cloth or plastic wrap, and let it rise in a warm place for about 1-1.5 hours, or until it has doubled in size.

4. Shape the Dough:

- **Pre-Shape:** Punch down the dough to release air. Turn it out onto a lightly floured surface and shape it into a loaf. You can also divide it into smaller pieces to make rolls if you prefer.
- **Final Shaping:** Place the shaped dough into a greased loaf pan or on a baking sheet. Cover it loosely and let it rise for another 30-45 minutes, or until it has risen noticeably.

5. Preheat the Oven:

- Preheat your oven to 350°F (175°C).

6. Bake the Bread:

- **Bake:** Place the loaf in the preheated oven and bake for 25-30 minutes, or until the bread is golden brown and sounds hollow when tapped on the bottom.

7. Cool the Bread:

- **Rest:** Remove the bread from the oven and let it cool in the pan for about 10 minutes. Transfer it to a wire rack to cool completely before slicing.

Pain au Lait is delightful on its own or with a spread of butter, jam, or even as a base for French toast. Enjoy the soft, slightly sweet flavor of this classic bread!

Pain au Cacao (Chocolate Bread)

Ingredients:

For the Dough:

- 500 grams all-purpose flour
- 50 grams cocoa powder (unsweetened)
- 100 grams sugar
- 10 grams salt
- 10 grams active dry yeast (or 15 grams fresh yeast)
- 250 ml whole milk (warm)
- 60 grams unsalted butter (softened)
- 1 large egg

For the Filling:

- 100 grams dark chocolate (chopped into small pieces or use chocolate chips)
- 50 grams sugar (optional, for extra sweetness)

For the Topping (Optional):

- 1 egg (beaten, for egg wash)
- A handful of chocolate chips or shavings

Instructions:

1. Prepare the Yeast:

- **Activate Yeast:** If using active dry yeast, dissolve it in the warm milk with a pinch of sugar and let it sit for 5-10 minutes until it becomes frothy. If using fresh yeast, crumble it into the milk and let it dissolve for a few minutes.

2. Mix the Dough:

- **Combine Dry Ingredients:** In a large mixing bowl, whisk together the flour, cocoa powder, sugar, and salt.
- **Add Wet Ingredients:** Make a well in the center of the dry ingredients and add the activated yeast mixture, egg, and softened butter. Mix until the dough starts to come together.
- **Knead:** Turn the dough onto a lightly floured surface and knead for about 10 minutes, or until it is smooth and elastic.

3. First Rise:

- **Bulk Fermentation:** Place the dough in a lightly oiled bowl, cover it with a damp cloth or plastic wrap, and let it rise in a warm place for about 1-1.5 hours, or until it has doubled in size.

4. Shape the Dough:

- **Pre-Shape:** Punch down the dough to release air. Turn it out onto a lightly floured surface and roll it into a rectangle (about 12x18 inches or 30x45 cm).
- **Add Filling:** Evenly sprinkle the chopped chocolate (and additional sugar, if using) over the dough.
- **Roll Up:** Roll the dough up tightly from the long side, like a jelly roll, and then place it seam-side down. You can shape it into a loaf or cut it into rolls if you prefer.
- **Place in Pan:** Place the rolled dough into a greased loaf pan or on a baking sheet, depending on your shape preference. Cover and let it rise for another 30-45 minutes.

5. Preheat the Oven:

- Preheat your oven to 350°F (175°C).

6. Bake the Bread:

- **Egg Wash and Topping:** Brush the top of the dough with the beaten egg for a glossy finish, and sprinkle with additional chocolate chips or shavings if desired.
- **Bake:** Place the loaf in the preheated oven and bake for 30-35 minutes, or until the bread is firm and sounds hollow when tapped on the bottom.

7. Cool the Bread:

- **Rest:** Remove the bread from the oven and let it cool in the pan for about 10 minutes. Transfer it to a wire rack to cool completely before slicing.

This chocolate bread is delicious on its own, or you can enjoy it with a spread of butter, jam, or even additional chocolate for a truly indulgent treat. Enjoy your homemade Pain au Cacao!

Pain à l'Ancienne (Old-fashioned Bread)

Ingredients:

- **500g (4 cups) all-purpose flour**
- **375ml (1.5 cups) water**
- **10g (2 tsp) salt**
- **1g (1/4 tsp) active dry yeast or instant yeast**

Instructions:

1. **Mix the Dough:**
    - In a large bowl, combine the flour and yeast. Add the water gradually, mixing until the dough starts to come together.
    - Add the salt and mix well. The dough will be quite sticky; this is normal.
2. **First Rise:**
    - Cover the bowl with plastic wrap or a damp cloth. Let it rise at room temperature for 12-16 hours. This long fermentation time is key to developing the flavor and texture.
3. **Shape the Dough:**
    - After the dough has risen and is bubbly, turn it out onto a floured surface. Gently shape it into a round loaf. Avoid overworking the dough; it should remain airy.
4. **Second Rise:**
    - Place the shaped dough onto a parchment-lined baking sheet or into a well-floured proofing basket. Cover and let it rise for about 1-2 hours, until it has visibly expanded.
5. **Preheat the Oven:**
    - About 30 minutes before baking, preheat your oven to 250°C (475°F). If you're using a Dutch oven or pizza stone, place it in the oven to preheat as well.
6. **Score the Bread:**

- Just before baking, use a sharp knife or razor blade to score the top of the loaf. This helps control how the bread expands as it bakes.

7. **Bake:**
    - If using a Dutch oven, carefully place the dough inside and cover it. Bake for 20 minutes, then remove the lid and bake for an additional 20-25 minutes, until the crust is deeply browned and the internal temperature of the bread reaches around 90°C (195°F).
    - If baking on a baking sheet or pizza stone, bake for about 30-35 minutes, until the crust is golden and the bread sounds hollow when tapped on the bottom.

8. **Cool:**
    - Let the bread cool on a wire rack before slicing. This allows the crumb to set and enhances the flavor.

Pain à l'Ancienne is fantastic on its own or as a base for sandwiches and toast. Enjoy the process and the delicious results!

Pain de Campagne au Levain (Country Sourdough)

Ingredients:

For the Sourdough Starter:

- **50g (1/2 cup) all-purpose flour**
- **50g (1/4 cup) water**
- **1 tablespoon of active sourdough starter or a small amount of commercial yeast (optional, if starting a new culture)**

For the Bread:

- **500g (4 cups) all-purpose flour or bread flour**
- **350g (1.5 cups) water**
- **100g (1/2 cup) sourdough starter (mature and active)**
- **10g (2 tsp) salt**

Instructions:

1. Prepare the Sourdough Starter:

- **If you already have a mature starter:** Feed it with equal parts flour and water and let it sit at room temperature for 4-6 hours, or until bubbly and active.
- **If starting from scratch:** Combine 50g flour and 50g water in a jar. Cover loosely and let it sit at room temperature. Feed it daily with equal parts flour and water for about 5-7 days until it becomes bubbly and doubles in size.

2. Autolyse:

- In a large bowl, combine 500g flour and 350g water. Mix until there are no dry spots. Let this mixture rest for 30 minutes to 1 hour. This step helps with dough hydration and gluten development.

3. Add Starter and Salt:

- After the autolyse, add 100g of your active sourdough starter and 10g salt to the dough. Mix thoroughly. You can use your hands or a spoon to incorporate everything.

4. Knead the Dough:

- Knead the dough on a lightly floured surface for about 10 minutes, or until it becomes smooth and elastic. Alternatively, you can use the stretch and fold method: stretch the dough and fold it over itself every 30 minutes for 2 hours.

5. First Rise:

- Place the dough in a lightly oiled bowl, cover it with plastic wrap or a damp cloth, and let it rise at room temperature for 4-6 hours, or until it has doubled in size.

6. Pre-shape and Rest:

- Turn the dough out onto a lightly floured surface. Gently shape it into a round or oval shape. Let it rest for about 20 minutes, covered with a cloth.

7. Shape the Dough:

- Shape the dough into its final form, either a round loaf or an oval batard. Place it seam-side up in a well-floured proofing basket or bowl lined with a floured cloth.

8. Second Rise:

- Cover the dough and let it rise for 1-2 hours, or until it has nearly doubled in size.

9. Preheat the Oven:

- Preheat your oven to 250°C (475°F). If using a Dutch oven or pizza stone, place it in the oven to preheat as well.

10. Score and Bake:

- Carefully transfer the dough to the preheated Dutch oven or pizza stone. Score the top with a sharp blade or knife to help it expand properly.
- Bake covered (if using a Dutch oven) for 20 minutes. Then, remove the cover and bake for an additional 20-25 minutes, or until the crust is deeply browned and the loaf sounds hollow when tapped on the bottom.

11. Cool:

- Allow the bread to cool completely on a wire rack before slicing. This helps the crumb set and enhances the flavor.

Tips:

- **Starter Health:** Make sure your sourdough starter is active and bubbly before using it. If it's been in the fridge, feed it and let it sit at room temperature for several hours before using.
- **Hydration:** Adjust the water slightly if you prefer a wetter or drier dough. A higher hydration dough tends to be more open and airy.

Enjoy your homemade Pain de Campagne au Levain!

Pain au Fromage (Cheese Bread)

Ingredients:

- 500g (4 cups) all-purpose or bread flour
- 300ml (1.25 cups) warm milk (about 40°C/105°F)
- 7g (2 tsp) active dry yeast or instant yeast
- 50g (1/4 cup) unsalted butter, softened
- 1 large egg
- 10g (2 tsp) salt
- 200g (2 cups) shredded cheese (e.g., Gruyère, Cheddar, or Emmental)
- Optional: 1/2 tsp garlic powder or dried herbs for extra flavor

Instructions:

1. **Activate the Yeast:**
   - In a small bowl, dissolve the yeast in the warm milk. Let it sit for about 5-10 minutes, or until it becomes frothy. This step is important for ensuring your yeast is active.
2. **Prepare the Dough:**
   - In a large mixing bowl, combine the flour and salt (and optional garlic powder or herbs if using).
   - Make a well in the center and pour in the yeast mixture, softened butter, and the egg.
   - Mix until a dough starts to form, then knead on a lightly floured surface for about 10 minutes, or until the dough is smooth and elastic.
3. **Incorporate the Cheese:**
   - Gently fold in the shredded cheese until evenly distributed throughout the dough. Be careful not to overwork it.
4. **First Rise:**
   - Place the dough in a lightly oiled bowl, cover with plastic wrap or a damp cloth, and let it rise in a warm place for about 1-2 hours, or until it has doubled in size.
5. **Shape the Dough:**
   - Turn the dough out onto a floured surface and shape it into a loaf or divide it into smaller rolls, depending on your preference.
   - Place the shaped dough onto a parchment-lined baking sheet or into a greased loaf pan.
6. **Second Rise:**
   - Cover the dough with a cloth and let it rise for about 30-60 minutes, or until it has puffed up and is nearly doubled in size.
7. **Preheat the Oven:**
   - Preheat your oven to 220°C (425°F).
8. **Bake:**
   - Bake the bread in the preheated oven for 25-30 minutes, or until the crust is golden brown and the loaf sounds hollow when tapped on the bottom.

- If you like a cheesier crust, you can sprinkle some additional cheese on top of the dough before baking.
9. **Cool:**
    - Allow the bread to cool on a wire rack before slicing. This helps the crumb set and improves the flavor.

Tips:

- **Cheese Choices:** Use cheeses that melt well, like Gruyère, Cheddar, or Emmental. You can also mix different cheeses for varied flavors.
- **Add-ins:** Feel free to experiment by adding cooked bacon, ham, or herbs to the dough for extra flavor.

Enjoy your homemade Pain au Fromage! It's perfect for a snack on its own or as a complement to soups and salads.

Pain au Romarin (Rosemary Bread)

Ingredients:

- 500g (4 cups) all-purpose or bread flour
- 300ml (1.25 cups) warm water (about 40°C/105°F)
- 7g (2 tsp) active dry yeast or instant yeast
- 10g (2 tsp) salt
- 3-4 tablespoons fresh rosemary leaves (finely chopped)
- 30ml (2 tbsp) olive oil
- Optional: 1 tablespoon honey or sugar (for a slightly sweeter bread)

Instructions:

1. **Activate the Yeast:**
    - In a small bowl, dissolve the yeast in the warm water. Let it sit for about 5-10 minutes, or until it becomes frothy. If you're using honey or sugar, add it to the water with the yeast.
2. **Prepare the Dough:**
    - In a large mixing bowl, combine the flour and salt. Add the chopped rosemary to the flour.
    - Make a well in the center and pour in the yeast mixture and olive oil.
    - Mix until a dough forms. If the dough feels too sticky, add a bit more flour as needed. If it's too dry, add a bit more water.
3. **Knead the Dough:**
    - Turn the dough out onto a floured surface and knead for about 10 minutes, or until the dough is smooth and elastic.
4. **First Rise:**

- Place the dough in a lightly oiled bowl, cover with plastic wrap or a damp cloth, and let it rise in a warm place for about 1-2 hours, or until it has doubled in size.
5. **Shape the Dough:**
    - Turn the dough out onto a floured surface and gently shape it into a loaf or divide it into smaller rolls.
    - Place the shaped dough onto a parchment-lined baking sheet or into a greased loaf pan.
6. **Second Rise:**
    - Cover the dough with a cloth and let it rise for about 30-60 minutes, or until it has puffed up and is nearly doubled in size.
7. **Preheat the Oven:**
    - Preheat your oven to 220°C (425°F).
8. **Bake:**
    - Optionally, brush the top of the dough with a little olive oil and sprinkle some additional rosemary on top.
    - Bake in the preheated oven for 25-30 minutes, or until the crust is golden brown and the loaf sounds hollow when tapped on the bottom.
9. **Cool:**
    - Allow the bread to cool on a wire rack before slicing. This helps the crumb set and enhances the flavor.

Tips:

- **Rosemary:** Fresh rosemary is best for this recipe, but dried rosemary can be used if fresh isn't available. Use less dried rosemary (about 1-2 tablespoons) since it's more concentrated.
- **Flavor Enhancements:** You can also add a bit of sea salt or coarse salt on top of the bread before baking for extra flavor and texture.
- **Storage:** Store the bread in an airtight container or plastic bag at room temperature for up to 3 days. It can also be frozen for longer storage.

Pain au Romarin is perfect with a variety of dishes, from soups and salads to just enjoying with a bit of butter. Enjoy baking and savoring your homemade rosemary bread!

Pain au Beurre (Butter Bread)

Ingredients:

- **500g (4 cups) all-purpose or bread flour**
- **300ml (1.25 cups) warm milk (about 40°C/105°F)**
- **7g (2 tsp) active dry yeast or instant yeast**
- **100g (1/2 cup) unsalted butter, softened**
- **50g (1/4 cup) sugar**
- **10g (2 tsp) salt**
- **1 large egg**
- **Optional: 1 egg yolk + 1 tablespoon milk for egg wash**

Instructions:

1. **Activate the Yeast:**
    - In a small bowl, dissolve the yeast in the warm milk. Let it sit for about 5-10 minutes, or until it becomes frothy.
2. **Prepare the Dough:**
    - In a large mixing bowl, combine the flour, sugar, and salt.
    - Make a well in the center and add the yeast mixture, softened butter, and egg.
    - Mix until a dough starts to form. If the dough is too sticky, add a bit more flour as needed. If it's too dry, add a bit more milk.
3. **Knead the Dough:**
    - Turn the dough out onto a floured surface and knead for about 10 minutes, or until the dough is smooth and elastic.
4. **First Rise:**
    - Place the dough in a lightly oiled bowl, cover with plastic wrap or a damp cloth, and let it rise in a warm place for about 1-2 hours, or until it has doubled in size.
5. **Shape the Dough:**
    - Turn the dough out onto a floured surface and shape it into a loaf or divide it into smaller pieces for rolls.
    - Place the shaped dough onto a parchment-lined baking sheet or into a greased loaf pan.
6. **Second Rise:**
    - Cover the dough with a cloth and let it rise for about 30-60 minutes, or until it has puffed up and is nearly doubled in size.
7. **Preheat the Oven:**
    - Preheat your oven to 220°C (425°F).
8. **Optional: Egg Wash:**
    - For a golden, shiny crust, mix 1 egg yolk with 1 tablespoon milk and brush it over the top of the dough before baking.
9. **Bake:**
    - Bake in the preheated oven for 25-30 minutes, or until the crust is golden brown and the loaf sounds hollow when tapped on the bottom.
10. **Cool:**

- Allow the bread to cool on a wire rack before slicing. This helps the crumb set and improves the flavor.

Tips:

- **Butter:** Use unsalted butter for a controlled flavor, but if you only have salted butter, you can adjust the added salt in the recipe accordingly.
- **Flavor Variations:** Add herbs, cheese, or a bit of cinnamon and sugar for different flavor profiles.
- **Storage:** Store the bread in an airtight container or plastic bag at room temperature for up to 3 days. It can also be frozen for longer storage.

Enjoy your homemade Pain au Beurre! It's a wonderfully rich and soft bread that pairs well with many different toppings or can be enjoyed on its own.

Pain au Miel (Honey Bread)

Ingredients:

- **500g (4 cups) all-purpose or bread flour**
- **300ml (1.25 cups) warm milk (about 40°C/105°F)**
- **7g (2 tsp) active dry yeast or instant yeast**
- **100g (1/3 cup) honey**
- **50g (1/4 cup) unsalted butter, softened**
- **10g (2 tsp) salt**
- **1 large egg**
- **Optional: 1 egg yolk + 1 tablespoon milk for egg wash**

Instructions:

1. **Activate the Yeast:**
   - In a small bowl, dissolve the yeast in the warm milk. Let it sit for about 5-10 minutes, or until it becomes frothy.
2. **Prepare the Dough:**
   - In a large mixing bowl, combine the flour and salt.
   - Make a well in the center and add the yeast mixture, honey, softened butter, and egg.
   - Mix until a dough starts to form. If the dough is too sticky, add a bit more flour. If it's too dry, add a bit more milk.
3. **Knead the Dough:**
   - Turn the dough out onto a floured surface and knead for about 10 minutes, or until the dough is smooth and elastic.
4. **First Rise:**
   - Place the dough in a lightly oiled bowl, cover with plastic wrap or a damp cloth, and let it rise in a warm place for about 1-2 hours, or until it has doubled in size.
5. **Shape the Dough:**
   - Turn the dough out onto a floured surface and shape it into a loaf or divide it into smaller pieces for rolls.
   - Place the shaped dough onto a parchment-lined baking sheet or into a greased loaf pan.
6. **Second Rise:**
   - Cover the dough with a cloth and let it rise for about 30-60 minutes, or until it has puffed up and is nearly doubled in size.
7. **Preheat the Oven:**
   - Preheat your oven to 220°C (425°F).
8. **Optional: Egg Wash:**
   - For a golden, shiny crust, mix 1 egg yolk with 1 tablespoon milk and brush it over the top of the dough before baking.
9. **Bake:**
   - Bake in the preheated oven for 25-30 minutes, or until the crust is golden brown and the loaf sounds hollow when tapped on the bottom.

10. **Cool:**
    - Allow the bread to cool on a wire rack before slicing. This helps the crumb set and improves the flavor.

Tips:

- **Honey:** Use good quality honey for the best flavor. You can also experiment with different types of honey for varied tastes.
- **Butter:** Ensure the butter is softened to mix well into the dough.
- **Flavor Variations:** Consider adding spices like cinnamon or nutmeg for extra warmth, or mix in nuts or dried fruit if you like.

Pain au Miel is a versatile and delicious bread with a subtle sweetness from the honey. Enjoy it fresh or toasted, and it's sure to be a hit with your family and friends!

Pain au Figues (Fig Bread)

Ingredients:

- **500g (4 cups) all-purpose or bread flour**
- **300ml (1.25 cups) warm water (about 40°C/105°F)**
- **7g (2 tsp) active dry yeast or instant yeast**
- **10g (2 tsp) salt**
- **100g (1 cup) dried figs, chopped**
- **30ml (2 tbsp) olive oil**
- **Optional: 1 tablespoon honey or sugar (for a slightly sweeter bread)**

Instructions:

1. **Prepare the Figs:**
   - Chop the dried figs into small pieces. If you like, you can soak them in a bit of warm water for about 10 minutes to soften them, then drain them before adding to the dough.
2. **Activate the Yeast:**
   - In a small bowl, dissolve the yeast in the warm water. Let it sit for about 5-10 minutes, or until it becomes frothy. If using honey or sugar, add it to the water with the yeast.
3. **Prepare the Dough:**
   - In a large mixing bowl, combine the flour and salt.
   - Make a well in the center and add the yeast mixture and olive oil.
   - Mix until a dough starts to form. If the dough is too sticky, add a bit more flour. If it's too dry, add a bit more water.
4. **Incorporate the Figs:**
   - Gently fold the chopped figs into the dough until evenly distributed.
5. **Knead the Dough:**

- Turn the dough out onto a floured surface and knead for about 10 minutes, or until the dough is smooth and elastic.
6. **First Rise:**
   - Place the dough in a lightly oiled bowl, cover with plastic wrap or a damp cloth, and let it rise in a warm place for about 1-2 hours, or until it has doubled in size.
7. **Shape the Dough:**
   - Turn the dough out onto a floured surface and shape it into a loaf or divide it into smaller pieces for rolls.
   - Place the shaped dough onto a parchment-lined baking sheet or into a greased loaf pan.
8. **Second Rise:**
   - Cover the dough with a cloth and let it rise for about 30-60 minutes, or until it has puffed up and is nearly doubled in size.
9. **Preheat the Oven:**
   - Preheat your oven to 220°C (425°F).
10. **Bake:**
    - Bake in the preheated oven for 25-30 minutes, or until the crust is golden brown and the loaf sounds hollow when tapped on the bottom.
11. **Cool:**
    - Allow the bread to cool on a wire rack before slicing. This helps the crumb set and enhances the flavor.

Tips:

- **Figs:** Use good quality dried figs. If they're very dry, soaking them will help make them softer and easier to incorporate into the dough.
- **Flavor Variations:** Add nuts such as walnuts or almonds for extra texture, or a bit of cinnamon or nutmeg for additional warmth.

Pain au Figues is a wonderful, unique bread with a sweet, fruity flavor from the figs. It's perfect for a special breakfast, a treat with tea, or as part of a cheese platter. Enjoy baking and savoring your homemade fig bread!

Pain au Cumin (Cumin Bread)

Ingredients:

- 500g (4 cups) all-purpose or bread flour
- 300ml (1.25 cups) warm water (about 40°C/105°F)
- 7g (2 tsp) active dry yeast or instant yeast
- 10g (2 tsp) salt
- 2 tablespoons cumin seeds
- 30ml (2 tbsp) olive oil
- Optional: 1 tablespoon honey or sugar (for a slightly sweeter bread)

Instructions:

1. **Toast the Cumin Seeds (Optional but recommended):**
   - In a dry skillet over medium heat, toast the cumin seeds until they are fragrant, about 1-2 minutes. Be careful not to burn them. Let them cool before adding to the dough.
2. **Activate the Yeast:**
   - In a small bowl, dissolve the yeast in the warm water. Let it sit for about 5-10 minutes, or until it becomes frothy. If you're using honey or sugar, add it to the water with the yeast.
3. **Prepare the Dough:**
   - In a large mixing bowl, combine the flour and salt.
   - Make a well in the center and add the yeast mixture and olive oil.
   - Mix until a dough starts to form. If the dough is too sticky, add a bit more flour. If it's too dry, add a bit more water.
4. **Incorporate the Cumin Seeds:**
   - Gently fold the toasted cumin seeds into the dough until evenly distributed.
5. **Knead the Dough:**
   - Turn the dough out onto a floured surface and knead for about 10 minutes, or until the dough is smooth and elastic.
6. **First Rise:**
   - Place the dough in a lightly oiled bowl, cover with plastic wrap or a damp cloth, and let it rise in a warm place for about 1-2 hours, or until it has doubled in size.
7. **Shape the Dough:**
   - Turn the dough out onto a floured surface and shape it into a loaf or divide it into smaller pieces for rolls.
   - Place the shaped dough onto a parchment-lined baking sheet or into a greased loaf pan.
8. **Second Rise:**
   - Cover the dough with a cloth and let it rise for about 30-60 minutes, or until it has puffed up and is nearly doubled in size.
9. **Preheat the Oven:**
   - Preheat your oven to 220°C (425°F).
10. **Bake:**

- Bake in the preheated oven for 25-30 minutes, or until the crust is golden brown and the loaf sounds hollow when tapped on the bottom.

11. **Cool:**
    - Allow the bread to cool on a wire rack before slicing. This helps the crumb set and improves the flavor.

Tips:

- **Cumin Seeds:** Toasting the cumin seeds enhances their flavor, but if you're short on time, you can use them raw.
- **Flavor Variations:** For additional complexity, you might add a small amount of ground coriander or a pinch of chili flakes.
- **Storage:** Store the bread in an airtight container or plastic bag at room temperature for up to 3 days. It can also be frozen for longer storage.

Pain au Cumin is a fragrant and delicious bread that adds a unique twist to your bread-baking repertoire. Enjoy the aromatic flavors and the delightful texture of your homemade cumin bread!

Pain au Jambon (Ham Bread)

Ingredients:

- **500g (4 cups) all-purpose or bread flour**
- **300ml (1.25 cups) warm milk (about 40°C/105°F)**
- **7g (2 tsp) active dry yeast or instant yeast**
- **50g (1/4 cup) unsalted butter, softened**
- **10g (2 tsp) salt**
- **1 large egg**
- **200g (7 oz) cooked ham, diced (use a good-quality ham for best flavor)**
- **Optional: 100g (1 cup) shredded cheese (e.g., Gruyère, Cheddar, or Emmental)**
- **Optional: 1 tablespoon honey or sugar (for a slightly sweeter bread)**

Instructions:

1. **Activate the Yeast:**
    - In a small bowl, dissolve the yeast in the warm milk. Let it sit for about 5-10 minutes, or until it becomes frothy. If you're using honey or sugar, add it to the milk with the yeast.
2. **Prepare the Dough:**
    - In a large mixing bowl, combine the flour and salt.
    - Make a well in the center and add the yeast mixture, softened butter, and egg.
    - Mix until a dough starts to form. If the dough is too sticky, add a bit more flour. If it's too dry, add a bit more milk.
3. **Incorporate the Ham and Cheese (Optional):**

- Gently fold the diced ham and shredded cheese (if using) into the dough until evenly distributed.
4. **Knead the Dough:**
    - Turn the dough out onto a floured surface and knead for about 10 minutes, or until the dough is smooth and elastic.
5. **First Rise:**
    - Place the dough in a lightly oiled bowl, cover with plastic wrap or a damp cloth, and let it rise in a warm place for about 1-2 hours, or until it has doubled in size.
6. **Shape the Dough:**
    - Turn the dough out onto a floured surface and shape it into a loaf or divide it into smaller pieces for rolls.
    - Place the shaped dough onto a parchment-lined baking sheet or into a greased loaf pan.
7. **Second Rise:**
    - Cover the dough with a cloth and let it rise for about 30-60 minutes, or until it has puffed up and is nearly doubled in size.
8. **Preheat the Oven:**
    - Preheat your oven to 220°C (425°F).
9. **Bake:**
    - Bake in the preheated oven for 25-30 minutes, or until the crust is golden brown and the loaf sounds hollow when tapped on the bottom.
10. **Cool:**
    - Allow the bread to cool on a wire rack before slicing. This helps the crumb set and improves the flavor.

Tips:

- **Ham:** Use good-quality cooked ham for the best flavor. You can also use leftover ham or ham from the deli. Ensure it's diced into small, even pieces for uniform distribution in the bread.
- **Cheese:** The cheese is optional but adds a nice richness and additional flavor. You can use any cheese that melts well.
- **Flavor Variations:** Add herbs like thyme or rosemary to the dough for extra flavor. You could also incorporate some finely chopped vegetables, like bell peppers or onions, if desired.

Pain au Jambon is a savory treat that's perfect for a hearty snack or meal. Enjoy your homemade ham bread with a variety of accompaniments or simply on its own!

Pain au Lard (Bacon Bread)

Ingredients:

- **500g (4 cups) all-purpose or bread flour**
- **300ml (1.25 cups) warm milk (about 40°C/105°F)**

- 7g (2 tsp) active dry yeast or instant yeast
- 50g (1/4 cup) unsalted butter, softened
- 10g (2 tsp) salt
- 1 large egg
- 200g (7 oz) bacon, diced (preferably thick-cut bacon)
- Optional: 100g (1 cup) shredded cheese (e.g., Cheddar or Gruyère)
- Optional: 1 tablespoon honey or sugar (for a slightly sweeter bread)

Instructions:

1. **Prepare the Bacon:**
   - In a skillet over medium heat, cook the diced bacon until crispy. Remove the bacon from the skillet and drain on paper towels to remove excess fat. Allow it to cool before adding to the dough.
2. **Activate the Yeast:**
   - In a small bowl, dissolve the yeast in the warm milk. Let it sit for about 5-10 minutes, or until it becomes frothy. If using honey or sugar, add it to the milk with the yeast.
3. **Prepare the Dough:**
   - In a large mixing bowl, combine the flour and salt.
   - Make a well in the center and add the yeast mixture, softened butter, and egg.
   - Mix until a dough starts to form. If the dough is too sticky, add a bit more flour. If it's too dry, add a bit more milk.
4. **Incorporate the Bacon and Cheese (Optional):**
   - Gently fold the cooked bacon and shredded cheese (if using) into the dough until evenly distributed.
5. **Knead the Dough:**
   - Turn the dough out onto a floured surface and knead for about 10 minutes, or until the dough is smooth and elastic.
6. **First Rise:**
   - Place the dough in a lightly oiled bowl, cover with plastic wrap or a damp cloth, and let it rise in a warm place for about 1-2 hours, or until it has doubled in size.
7. **Shape the Dough:**
   - Turn the dough out onto a floured surface and shape it into a loaf or divide it into smaller pieces for rolls.
   - Place the shaped dough onto a parchment-lined baking sheet or into a greased loaf pan.
8. **Second Rise:**
   - Cover the dough with a cloth and let it rise for about 30-60 minutes, or until it has puffed up and is nearly doubled in size.
9. **Preheat the Oven:**
   - Preheat your oven to 220°C (425°F).
10. **Bake:**

- Bake in the preheated oven for 25-30 minutes, or until the crust is golden brown and the loaf sounds hollow when tapped on the bottom.
11. **Cool:**
    - Allow the bread to cool on a wire rack before slicing. This helps the crumb set and improves the flavor.

Tips:

- **Bacon:** For best results, use good-quality bacon and make sure it's crispy before adding it to the dough to avoid excess grease.
- **Cheese:** Adding cheese is optional but enhances the flavor and richness of the bread.
- **Flavor Variations:** You can add finely chopped herbs like thyme or rosemary to the dough for additional flavor.

Pain au Lard is a hearty and flavorful bread that's sure to be a hit with anyone who loves bacon. Enjoy it fresh out of the oven or toasted with a bit of butter for a delicious treat!

Pain aux Olives (Olive Bread)

Ingredients:

- **500g (4 cups) all-purpose or bread flour**
- **300ml (1.25 cups) warm water (about 40°C/105°F)**
- **7g (2 tsp) active dry yeast or instant yeast**
- **10g (2 tsp) salt**
- **100g (3.5 oz) pitted olives (green, black, or a mix), chopped**
- **30ml (2 tbsp) olive oil**
- **Optional: 1 tablespoon honey or sugar (for a slightly sweeter bread)**

Instructions:

1. **Prepare the Olives:**
    - Chop the olives into small pieces. If they're very salty or briny, you may want to rinse them briefly and pat them dry to reduce the saltiness in the bread.
2. **Activate the Yeast:**
    - In a small bowl, dissolve the yeast in the warm water. Let it sit for about 5-10 minutes, or until it becomes frothy. If using honey or sugar, add it to the water with the yeast.
3. **Prepare the Dough:**
    - In a large mixing bowl, combine the flour and salt.
    - Make a well in the center and add the yeast mixture and olive oil.
    - Mix until a dough starts to form. If the dough is too sticky, add a bit more flour. If it's too dry, add a bit more water.
4. **Incorporate the Olives:**
    - Gently fold the chopped olives into the dough until evenly distributed.

5. **Knead the Dough:**
   - Turn the dough out onto a floured surface and knead for about 10 minutes, or until the dough is smooth and elastic.
6. **First Rise:**
   - Place the dough in a lightly oiled bowl, cover with plastic wrap or a damp cloth, and let it rise in a warm place for about 1-2 hours, or until it has doubled in size.
7. **Shape the Dough:**
   - Turn the dough out onto a floured surface and shape it into a loaf or divide it into smaller pieces for rolls.
   - Place the shaped dough onto a parchment-lined baking sheet or into a greased loaf pan.
8. **Second Rise:**
   - Cover the dough with a cloth and let it rise for about 30-60 minutes, or until it has puffed up and is nearly doubled in size.
9. **Preheat the Oven:**
   - Preheat your oven to 220°C (425°F).
10. **Bake:**
    - Bake in the preheated oven for 25-30 minutes, or until the crust is golden brown and the loaf sounds hollow when tapped on the bottom.
11. **Cool:**
    - Allow the bread to cool on a wire rack before slicing. This helps the crumb set and improves the flavor.

Tips:

- **Olives:** Use your favorite type of olives. Black olives tend to be a bit milder, while green olives can add a tangier flavor. You can also experiment with marinated or stuffed olives for a different taste.
- **Flavor Variations:** Consider adding herbs like rosemary or thyme to the dough for extra flavor. You might also sprinkle some sea salt on top of the dough before baking for added texture and flavor.
- **Storage:** Store the bread in an airtight container or plastic bag at room temperature for up to 3 days. It can also be frozen for longer storage.

Pain aux Olives is a versatile and tasty bread that pairs wonderfully with a variety of dishes. Enjoy the Mediterranean flavors and the delightful texture of your homemade olive bread!

Pain aux Noix et Fruits Secs (Nut and Dried Fruit Bread)

Ingredients:

- **500g (4 cups) all-purpose or bread flour**
- **300ml (1.25 cups) warm water (about 40°C/105°F)**
- **7g (2 tsp) active dry yeast or instant yeast**
- **10g (2 tsp) salt**

- 100g (3.5 oz) mixed nuts (e.g., walnuts, pecans, almonds), roughly chopped
- 100g (3.5 oz) dried fruit (e.g., raisins, dried apricots, cranberries), chopped if large
- 30ml (2 tbsp) olive oil or melted butter
- 1 large egg (optional, for egg wash)
- Optional: 1 tablespoon honey or sugar (for a slightly sweeter bread)

Instructions:

1. **Prepare the Nuts and Dried Fruit:**
    - Roughly chop the nuts and dried fruit into bite-sized pieces. If the dried fruit is very dry or tough, soak it in a bit of warm water for about 10 minutes, then drain and pat dry before adding it to the dough.
2. **Activate the Yeast:**
    - In a small bowl, dissolve the yeast in the warm water. Let it sit for about 5-10 minutes, or until it becomes frothy. If using honey or sugar, add it to the water with the yeast.
3. **Prepare the Dough:**
    - In a large mixing bowl, combine the flour and salt.
    - Make a well in the center and add the yeast mixture and olive oil or melted butter.
    - Mix until a dough starts to form. If the dough is too sticky, add a bit more flour. If it's too dry, add a bit more water.
4. **Incorporate the Nuts and Dried Fruit:**
    - Gently fold the chopped nuts and dried fruit into the dough until evenly distributed.
5. **Knead the Dough:**
    - Turn the dough out onto a floured surface and knead for about 10 minutes, or until the dough is smooth and elastic.
6. **First Rise:**
    - Place the dough in a lightly oiled bowl, cover with plastic wrap or a damp cloth, and let it rise in a warm place for about 1-2 hours, or until it has doubled in size.
7. **Shape the Dough:**
    - Turn the dough out onto a floured surface and shape it into a loaf or divide it into smaller pieces for rolls.
    - Place the shaped dough onto a parchment-lined baking sheet or into a greased loaf pan.
8. **Second Rise:**
    - Cover the dough with a cloth and let it rise for about 30-60 minutes, or until it has puffed up and is nearly doubled in size.
9. **Preheat the Oven:**
    - Preheat your oven to 220°C (425°F).
10. **Optional: Egg Wash:**
    - For a golden, shiny crust, mix 1 egg with a tablespoon of water and brush it over the top of the dough before baking.
11. **Bake:**

- Bake in the preheated oven for 25-30 minutes, or until the crust is golden brown and the loaf sounds hollow when tapped on the bottom.

12. **Cool:**
    - Allow the bread to cool on a wire rack before slicing. This helps the crumb set and improves the flavor.

Tips:

- **Nuts and Fruit:** Use a mix of your favorite nuts and dried fruits. Feel free to experiment with different combinations for varied flavors.
- **Flavor Variations:** You can add spices like cinnamon or nutmeg to the dough for additional warmth. A bit of orange zest or lemon zest can also complement the dried fruit nicely.
- **Storage:** Store the bread in an airtight container or plastic bag at room temperature for up to 3 days. It can also be frozen for longer storage.

Pain aux Noix et Fruits Secs is a versatile and delicious bread that pairs well with a variety of foods. Enjoy the rich flavors and hearty texture of this homemade nut and dried fruit bread!

Pain au Pesto (Pesto Bread)

Ingredients:

- **500g (4 cups) all-purpose or bread flour**
- **300ml (1.25 cups) warm water (about 40°C/105°F)**
- **7g (2 tsp) active dry yeast or instant yeast**
- **10g (2 tsp) salt**
- **60g (1/4 cup) pesto (store-bought or homemade)**
- **30ml (2 tbsp) olive oil**
- **1 large egg (optional, for egg wash)**
- **Optional: 50g (1/2 cup) grated Parmesan cheese or another hard cheese**

Instructions:

1. **Activate the Yeast:**
   - In a small bowl, dissolve the yeast in the warm water. Let it sit for about 5-10 minutes, or until it becomes frothy. If using honey or sugar, add it to the water with the yeast.
2. **Prepare the Dough:**
   - In a large mixing bowl, combine the flour and salt.
   - Make a well in the center and add the yeast mixture, pesto, and olive oil.
   - Mix until a dough starts to form. If the dough is too sticky, add a bit more flour. If it's too dry, add a bit more water.
3. **Knead the Dough:**

- Turn the dough out onto a floured surface and knead for about 10 minutes, or until the dough is smooth and elastic.
4. **First Rise:**
    - Place the dough in a lightly oiled bowl, cover with plastic wrap or a damp cloth, and let it rise in a warm place for about 1-2 hours, or until it has doubled in size.
5. **Shape the Dough:**
    - Turn the dough out onto a floured surface and shape it into a loaf or divide it into smaller pieces for rolls.
    - If using cheese, sprinkle it over the dough and fold it in or shape the dough to include it.
    - Place the shaped dough onto a parchment-lined baking sheet or into a greased loaf pan.
6. **Second Rise:**
    - Cover the dough with a cloth and let it rise for about 30-60 minutes, or until it has puffed up and is nearly doubled in size.
7. **Preheat the Oven:**
    - Preheat your oven to 220°C (425°F).
8. **Optional: Egg Wash:**
    - For a golden, shiny crust, mix 1 egg with a tablespoon of water and brush it over the top of the dough before baking.
9. **Bake:**
    - Bake in the preheated oven for 25-30 minutes, or until the crust is golden brown and the loaf sounds hollow when tapped on the bottom.
10. **Cool:**
    - Allow the bread to cool on a wire rack before slicing. This helps the crumb set and improves the flavor.

Tips:

- **Pesto:** Use your favorite pesto recipe or store-bought pesto. You can use basil pesto, sun-dried tomato pesto, or any other variety you like.
- **Cheese:** Adding cheese to the dough enhances the flavor and creates a delicious, savory loaf. Parmesan, Gruyère, or another hard cheese works well.
- **Flavor Variations:** You can incorporate other herbs or spices into the dough to complement the pesto, or add nuts like pine nuts for extra texture.

Pain au Pesto is a versatile and flavorful bread that's sure to impress. Enjoy the rich taste of pesto in every slice of this homemade bread!

Pain à l'ail (Garlic Bread)

Ingredients:

- **500g (4 cups) all-purpose or bread flour**
- **300ml (1.25 cups) warm water (about 40°C/105°F)**
- **7g (2 tsp) active dry yeast or instant yeast**
- **10g (2 tsp) salt**
- **30ml (2 tbsp) olive oil**
- **1-2 heads of garlic (to taste)**
- **100g (1/2 cup) unsalted butter, softened**
- **2-3 tablespoons fresh parsley, finely chopped**
- **Optional: 50g (1/2 cup) grated Parmesan cheese**
- **Optional: 1 tablespoon honey or sugar (for a slightly sweeter bread)**

Instructions:

1. **Prepare the Garlic:**
   - Peel and finely mince or crush the garlic cloves. For a milder garlic flavor, you can roast the garlic first. To roast, wrap the garlic in foil and bake at 200°C (400°F) for about 30 minutes, then squeeze the cloves out and mash them.
2. **Activate the Yeast:**
   - In a small bowl, dissolve the yeast in the warm water. Let it sit for about 5-10 minutes, or until it becomes frothy. If using honey or sugar, add it to the water with the yeast.
3. **Prepare the Dough:**
   - In a large mixing bowl, combine the flour and salt.
   - Make a well in the center and add the yeast mixture and olive oil.
   - Mix until a dough starts to form. If the dough is too sticky, add a bit more flour. If it's too dry, add a bit more water.
4. **Knead the Dough:**
   - Turn the dough out onto a floured surface and knead for about 10 minutes, or until the dough is smooth and elastic.
5. **First Rise:**
   - Place the dough in a lightly oiled bowl, cover with plastic wrap or a damp cloth, and let it rise in a warm place for about 1-2 hours, or until it has doubled in size.
6. **Prepare the Garlic Butter:**
   - In a small bowl, mix the softened butter with the minced or roasted garlic, and finely chopped parsley. If using Parmesan cheese, mix it in as well. Adjust the amount of garlic to your taste.
7. **Shape the Dough:**
   - Turn the dough out onto a floured surface and shape it into a loaf or divide it into smaller pieces for rolls. You can also shape it into a baguette or any shape you prefer.
   - Place the shaped dough onto a parchment-lined baking sheet or into a greased loaf pan.

8. **Second Rise:**
   - Cover the dough with a cloth and let it rise for about 30-60 minutes, or until it has puffed up and is nearly doubled in size.
9. **Preheat the Oven:**
   - Preheat your oven to 220°C (425°F).
10. **Apply Garlic Butter:**
    - Spread the garlic butter mixture generously over the top of the risen dough.
11. **Bake:**
    - Bake in the preheated oven for 25-30 minutes, or until the crust is golden brown and the loaf sounds hollow when tapped on the bottom.
12. **Cool:**
    - Allow the bread to cool on a wire rack before slicing. This helps the crumb set and enhances the flavor.

Tips:

- **Garlic Amount:** Adjust the amount of garlic to suit your taste. More garlic will give a stronger flavor, while less will be milder.
- **Herbs:** Feel free to add other herbs to the garlic butter, such as rosemary or thyme, for additional flavor.
- **Cheese:** Adding Parmesan to the garlic butter mixture adds a nice savory touch. You can also sprinkle some on top of the bread before baking for extra flavor.

Pain à l'ail is a classic and irresistible bread that's always a hit. Enjoy the rich garlic flavor and the delightful texture of this homemade bread!

Pain au Thym (Thyme Bread)

Ingredients:

- **500g (4 cups) all-purpose or bread flour**
- **300ml (1.25 cups) warm water (about 40°C/105°F)**
- **7g (2 tsp) active dry yeast or instant yeast**
- **10g (2 tsp) salt**
- **30ml (2 tbsp) olive oil**
- **2-3 tablespoons fresh thyme leaves (or 1-2 tablespoons dried thyme)**
- **Optional: 1 tablespoon honey or sugar (for a slightly sweeter bread)**

Instructions:

1. **Activate the Yeast:**
   - In a small bowl, dissolve the yeast in the warm water. Let it sit for about 5-10 minutes, or until it becomes frothy. If using honey or sugar, add it to the water with the yeast.
2. **Prepare the Dough:**

- In a large mixing bowl, combine the flour and salt.
- Make a well in the center and add the yeast mixture and olive oil.
- Mix until a dough starts to form. If the dough is too sticky, add a bit more flour. If it's too dry, add a bit more water.

3. **Incorporate the Thyme:**
   - Gently fold the fresh thyme leaves (or dried thyme) into the dough until evenly distributed.
4. **Knead the Dough:**
   - Turn the dough out onto a floured surface and knead for about 10 minutes, or until the dough is smooth and elastic.
5. **First Rise:**
   - Place the dough in a lightly oiled bowl, cover with plastic wrap or a damp cloth, and let it rise in a warm place for about 1-2 hours, or until it has doubled in size.
6. **Shape the Dough:**
   - Turn the dough out onto a floured surface and shape it into a loaf or divide it into smaller pieces for rolls.
   - Place the shaped dough onto a parchment-lined baking sheet or into a greased loaf pan.
7. **Second Rise:**
   - Cover the dough with a cloth and let it rise for about 30-60 minutes, or until it has puffed up and is nearly doubled in size.
8. **Preheat the Oven:**
   - Preheat your oven to 220°C (425°F).
9. **Bake:**
   - Bake in the preheated oven for 25-30 minutes, or until the crust is golden brown and the loaf sounds hollow when tapped on the bottom.
10. **Cool:**
    - Allow the bread to cool on a wire rack before slicing. This helps the crumb set and improves the flavor.

Tips:

- **Thyme:** Fresh thyme will give a more vibrant flavor compared to dried thyme, but either works well. If using dried thyme, you might want to use a bit less, as dried herbs are more concentrated.
- **Flavor Variations:** You can add other herbs or spices to the dough to complement the thyme. A bit of rosemary or some garlic can add extra depth of flavor.
- **Storage:** Store the bread in an airtight container or plastic bag at room temperature for up to 3 days. It can also be frozen for longer storage.

Pain au Thym is a wonderfully aromatic bread that pairs beautifully with a wide range of dishes. Enjoy the subtle yet distinctive flavor of thyme in every slice of this homemade bread!

Pain aux Herbes (Herb Bread)

Ingredients:

- 500g (4 cups) all-purpose or bread flour
- 300ml (1.25 cups) warm water (about 40°C/105°F)
- 7g (2 tsp) active dry yeast or instant yeast
- 10g (2 tsp) salt
- 30ml (2 tbsp) olive oil
- 2-3 tablespoons mixed fresh herbs (e.g., rosemary, thyme, basil, parsley) or 1-2 tablespoons dried herbs
- Optional: 1 tablespoon honey or sugar (for a slightly sweeter bread)

Instructions:

1. **Prepare the Herbs:**
   - If using fresh herbs, chop them finely. If using dried herbs, you can use them as they are. A mix of your favorite herbs will work well.
2. **Activate the Yeast:**
   - In a small bowl, dissolve the yeast in the warm water. Let it sit for about 5-10 minutes, or until it becomes frothy. If using honey or sugar, add it to the water with the yeast.
3. **Prepare the Dough:**
   - In a large mixing bowl, combine the flour and salt.
   - Make a well in the center and add the yeast mixture and olive oil.
   - Mix until a dough starts to form. If the dough is too sticky, add a bit more flour. If it's too dry, add a bit more water.
4. **Incorporate the Herbs:**
   - Gently fold the chopped fresh herbs (or dried herbs) into the dough until evenly distributed.
5. **Knead the Dough:**
   - Turn the dough out onto a floured surface and knead for about 10 minutes, or until the dough is smooth and elastic.
6. **First Rise:**
   - Place the dough in a lightly oiled bowl, cover with plastic wrap or a damp cloth, and let it rise in a warm place for about 1-2 hours, or until it has doubled in size.
7. **Shape the Dough:**
   - Turn the dough out onto a floured surface and shape it into a loaf or divide it into smaller pieces for rolls.
   - Place the shaped dough onto a parchment-lined baking sheet or into a greased loaf pan.
8. **Second Rise:**
   - Cover the dough with a cloth and let it rise for about 30-60 minutes, or until it has puffed up and is nearly doubled in size.
9. **Preheat the Oven:**
   - Preheat your oven to 220°C (425°F).

10. **Bake:**
    - Bake in the preheated oven for 25-30 minutes, or until the crust is golden brown and the loaf sounds hollow when tapped on the bottom.
11. **Cool:**
    - Allow the bread to cool on a wire rack before slicing. This helps the crumb set and enhances the flavor.

Tips:

- **Herb Combinations:** You can experiment with different combinations of herbs based on your preference. Fresh herbs generally have a more vibrant flavor, while dried herbs are more concentrated.
- **Flavor Variations:** Consider adding garlic or cheese to the dough for additional flavor. A sprinkle of sea salt on top before baking can also enhance the taste.
- **Storage:** Store the bread in an airtight container or plastic bag at room temperature for up to 3 days. It can also be frozen for longer storage.

Pain aux Herbes is a versatile and aromatic bread that can elevate many dishes or stand alone as a flavorful treat. Enjoy the fresh, herby aroma and taste of this homemade bread!

Pain au Safran (Saffron Bread)

Ingredients:

- 500g (4 cups) all-purpose or bread flour
- 300ml (1.25 cups) warm water (about 40°C/105°F)
- 7g (2 tsp) active dry yeast or instant yeast
- 10g (2 tsp) salt
- 30ml (2 tbsp) olive oil or melted butter
- 1/2 teaspoon saffron threads
- 1 tablespoon honey or sugar (optional, for a slightly sweeter bread)
- 1 large egg (optional, for egg wash)
- Optional: 50g (1/2 cup) raisins or currants for added sweetness

Instructions:

1. **Prepare the Saffron:**
    - Place the saffron threads in a small bowl and add 2 tablespoons of warm water. Let it steep for about 10 minutes to release its color and flavor. You can also lightly crush the threads before steeping to enhance the flavor extraction.
2. **Activate the Yeast:**
    - In a small bowl, dissolve the yeast in the warm water. Let it sit for about 5-10 minutes, or until it becomes frothy. If using honey or sugar, add it to the water with the yeast.
3. **Prepare the Dough:**

- In a large mixing bowl, combine the flour and salt.
- Make a well in the center and add the yeast mixture, saffron infusion (including the water), and olive oil or melted butter.
- Mix until a dough starts to form. If the dough is too sticky, add a bit more flour. If it's too dry, add a bit more water.

4. **Knead the Dough:**
    - Turn the dough out onto a floured surface and knead for about 10 minutes, or until the dough is smooth and elastic. If using raisins or currants, knead them in during this step.
5. **First Rise:**
    - Place the dough in a lightly oiled bowl, cover with plastic wrap or a damp cloth, and let it rise in a warm place for about 1-2 hours, or until it has doubled in size.
6. **Shape the Dough:**
    - Turn the dough out onto a floured surface and shape it into a loaf or divide it into smaller pieces for rolls.
    - Place the shaped dough onto a parchment-lined baking sheet or into a greased loaf pan.
7. **Second Rise:**
    - Cover the dough with a cloth and let it rise for about 30-60 minutes, or until it has puffed up and is nearly doubled in size.
8. **Preheat the Oven:**
    - Preheat your oven to 220°C (425°F).
9. **Optional: Egg Wash:**
    - For a golden, shiny crust, mix 1 egg with a tablespoon of water and brush it over the top of the dough before baking.
10. **Bake:**
    - Bake in the preheated oven for 25-30 minutes, or until the crust is golden brown and the loaf sounds hollow when tapped on the bottom.
11. **Cool:**
    - Allow the bread to cool on a wire rack before slicing. This helps the crumb set and enhances the flavor.

Tips:

- **Saffron:** Saffron is a potent ingredient, so a little goes a long way. Be sure to steep it properly to get the most out of its flavor and color.
- **Flavor Variations:** If you enjoy a slightly sweet bread, adding raisins or currants can complement the saffron flavor nicely.
- **Storage:** Store the bread in an airtight container or plastic bag at room temperature for up to 3 days. It can also be frozen for longer storage.

Pain au Safran is a unique and luxurious bread that brings a touch of elegance to your baking. Enjoy the beautiful color and rich flavor of this homemade saffron bread!

Pain au Citron (Lemon Bread)

Ingredients:

- **500g (4 cups) all-purpose or bread flour**
- **300ml (1.25 cups) warm water (about 40°C/105°F)**
- **7g (2 tsp) active dry yeast or instant yeast**
- **10g (2 tsp) salt**
- **30ml (2 tbsp) olive oil or melted butter**
- **Zest of 1 large lemon**
- **2 tablespoons fresh lemon juice**
- **1 tablespoon honey or sugar (optional, for a slightly sweeter bread)**
- **Optional: 50g (1/2 cup) lemon glaze (for a sweet finish)**

Instructions:

1. **Activate the Yeast:**
   - In a small bowl, dissolve the yeast in the warm water. Let it sit for about 5-10 minutes, or until it becomes frothy. If using honey or sugar, add it to the water with the yeast.
2. **Prepare the Dough:**
   - In a large mixing bowl, combine the flour and salt.
   - Make a well in the center and add the yeast mixture, olive oil or melted butter, lemon zest, and lemon juice.
   - Mix until a dough starts to form. If the dough is too sticky, add a bit more flour. If it's too dry, add a bit more water.
3. **Knead the Dough:**
   - Turn the dough out onto a floured surface and knead for about 10 minutes, or until the dough is smooth and elastic.
4. **First Rise:**
   - Place the dough in a lightly oiled bowl, cover with plastic wrap or a damp cloth, and let it rise in a warm place for about 1-2 hours, or until it has doubled in size.
5. **Shape the Dough:**
   - Turn the dough out onto a floured surface and shape it into a loaf or divide it into smaller pieces for rolls.
   - Place the shaped dough onto a parchment-lined baking sheet or into a greased loaf pan.
6. **Second Rise:**
   - Cover the dough with a cloth and let it rise for about 30-60 minutes, or until it has puffed up and is nearly doubled in size.
7. **Preheat the Oven:**
   - Preheat your oven to 220°C (425°F).
8. **Bake:**
   - Bake in the preheated oven for 25-30 minutes, or until the crust is golden brown and the loaf sounds hollow when tapped on the bottom.
9. **Optional: Lemon Glaze:**

- While the bread is baking, you can prepare a lemon glaze by mixing 1 cup powdered sugar with 2-3 tablespoons lemon juice. Drizzle this glaze over the bread once it's cooled.

10. **Cool:**
    - Allow the bread to cool on a wire rack before slicing. This helps the crumb set and enhances the flavor.

Tips:

- **Lemon Zest and Juice:** Make sure to use fresh lemon zest and juice for the best flavor. The zest provides a fragrant, intense lemon flavor while the juice adds moisture and tang.
- **Glaze:** The optional lemon glaze adds a sweet and tangy finish, but you can skip it if you prefer a less sweet bread.
- **Storage:** Store the bread in an airtight container or plastic bag at room temperature for up to 3 days. It can also be frozen for longer storage.

Pain au Citron is a delightful bread that brings a burst of citrusy freshness to your baking repertoire. Enjoy the tangy flavor and light texture of this homemade lemon bread!

Pain aux Pommes (Apple Bread)

Ingredients:

- **500g (4 cups) all-purpose or bread flour**
- **300ml (1.25 cups) warm water (about 40°C/105°F)**
- **7g (2 tsp) active dry yeast or instant yeast**
- **10g (2 tsp) salt**
- **30ml (2 tbsp) olive oil or melted butter**
- **1 large apple (such as Granny Smith, Honeycrisp, or your preferred variety)**
- **1 tablespoon honey or sugar (optional, for a slightly sweeter bread)**
- **1 teaspoon ground cinnamon (optional, for added flavor)**
- **1/4 teaspoon ground nutmeg (optional, for added flavor)**
- **Optional: 50g (1/2 cup) chopped nuts (such as walnuts or pecans) or raisins**

Instructions:

1. **Prepare the Apple:**
   - Peel, core, and finely dice the apple. If you prefer, you can lightly sauté the apple pieces in a pan with a bit of butter or oil and a sprinkle of cinnamon and sugar until they are tender. This step enhances the flavor and prevents the apples from being too crunchy in the bread.
2. **Activate the Yeast:**

- In a small bowl, dissolve the yeast in the warm water. Let it sit for about 5-10 minutes, or until it becomes frothy. If using honey or sugar, add it to the water with the yeast.
3. **Prepare the Dough:**
    - In a large mixing bowl, combine the flour and salt.
    - Make a well in the center and add the yeast mixture and olive oil or melted butter.
    - Mix until a dough starts to form. If the dough is too sticky, add a bit more flour. If it's too dry, add a bit more water.
4. **Incorporate the Apples and Optional Ingredients:**
    - Gently fold the diced apples into the dough. If using, add the cinnamon, nutmeg, nuts, and raisins at this stage. Mix until evenly distributed.
5. **Knead the Dough:**
    - Turn the dough out onto a floured surface and knead for about 10 minutes, or until the dough is smooth and elastic.
6. **First Rise:**
    - Place the dough in a lightly oiled bowl, cover with plastic wrap or a damp cloth, and let it rise in a warm place for about 1-2 hours, or until it has doubled in size.
7. **Shape the Dough:**
    - Turn the dough out onto a floured surface and shape it into a loaf or divide it into smaller pieces for rolls.
    - Place the shaped dough onto a parchment-lined baking sheet or into a greased loaf pan.
8. **Second Rise:**
    - Cover the dough with a cloth and let it rise for about 30-60 minutes, or until it has puffed up and is nearly doubled in size.
9. **Preheat the Oven:**
    - Preheat your oven to 220°C (425°F).
10. **Bake:**
    - Bake in the preheated oven for 25-30 minutes, or until the crust is golden brown and the loaf sounds hollow when tapped on the bottom.
11. **Cool:**
    - Allow the bread to cool on a wire rack before slicing. This helps the crumb set and enhances the flavor.

Tips:

- **Apple Variety:** Choose an apple variety that holds its shape well during baking, such as Granny Smith or Honeycrisp. Softer apples can become mushy in the bread.
- **Flavor Variations:** Adding spices like cinnamon and nutmeg enhances the apple flavor and gives the bread a warm, comforting aroma.
- **Storage:** Store the bread in an airtight container or plastic bag at room temperature for up to 3 days. It can also be frozen for longer storage.

Pain aux Pommes is a delightful bread that combines the sweetness and moisture of apples with the comforting texture of homemade bread. Enjoy the lovely apple flavor and the wonderful aroma of this freshly baked bread!

Pain au Curry (Curry Bread)

Ingredients:

- **500g (4 cups) all-purpose or bread flour**
- **300ml (1.25 cups) warm water (about 40°C/105°F)**
- **7g (2 tsp) active dry yeast or instant yeast**
- **10g (2 tsp) salt**
- **30ml (2 tbsp) olive oil or melted butter**
- **2-3 tablespoons curry powder (adjust to taste)**
- **Optional: 1 tablespoon honey or sugar (for a slightly sweeter bread)**
- **Optional: 1 small onion, finely chopped (sautéed until soft)**
- **Optional: 50g (1/2 cup) raisins or chopped nuts for added texture**

Instructions:

1. **Activate the Yeast:**
   - In a small bowl, dissolve the yeast in the warm water. Let it sit for about 5-10 minutes, or until it becomes frothy. If using honey or sugar, add it to the water with the yeast.
2. **Prepare the Dough:**
   - In a large mixing bowl, combine the flour, salt, and curry powder.
   - Make a well in the center and add the yeast mixture and olive oil or melted butter.
   - Mix until a dough starts to form. If the dough is too sticky, add a bit more flour. If it's too dry, add a bit more water.
3. **Incorporate Optional Ingredients:**
   - If using, gently fold in the sautéed onion, raisins, or nuts into the dough.
4. **Knead the Dough:**
   - Turn the dough out onto a floured surface and knead for about 10 minutes, or until the dough is smooth and elastic.
5. **First Rise:**
   - Place the dough in a lightly oiled bowl, cover with plastic wrap or a damp cloth, and let it rise in a warm place for about 1-2 hours, or until it has doubled in size.
6. **Shape the Dough:**
   - Turn the dough out onto a floured surface and shape it into a loaf or divide it into smaller pieces for rolls.
   - Place the shaped dough onto a parchment-lined baking sheet or into a greased loaf pan.
7. **Second Rise:**

- Cover the dough with a cloth and let it rise for about 30-60 minutes, or until it has puffed up and is nearly doubled in size.

8. **Preheat the Oven:**
   - Preheat your oven to 220°C (425°F).
9. **Bake:**
   - Bake in the preheated oven for 25-30 minutes, or until the crust is golden brown and the loaf sounds hollow when tapped on the bottom.
10. **Cool:**
    - Allow the bread to cool on a wire rack before slicing. This helps the crumb set and enhances the flavor.

Tips:

- **Curry Powder:** Adjust the amount of curry powder based on your taste preference. Different curry powders can vary in intensity, so start with a smaller amount and add more if desired.
- **Optional Ingredients:** Adding sautéed onions, raisins, or nuts can provide additional flavor and texture, but these are optional.
- **Storage:** Store the bread in an airtight container or plastic bag at room temperature for up to 3 days. It can also be frozen for longer storage.

Pain au Curry is a flavorful and aromatic bread that adds a unique twist to traditional bread recipes. Enjoy the delightful curry flavor in every slice of this homemade bread!

Pain au Chocolat (Chocolate-filled Bread)

Ingredients:

- **500g (4 cups) all-purpose or bread flour**
- **300ml (1.25 cups) warm water (about 40°C/105°F)**
- **7g (2 tsp) active dry yeast or instant yeast**
- **10g (2 tsp) salt**
- **30ml (2 tbsp) olive oil or melted butter**
- **1 tablespoon honey or sugar (optional, for a slightly sweeter dough)**
- **100-150g (3.5-5 oz) good-quality chocolate (dark, milk, or semi-sweet), cut into small pieces or use chocolate chips**

Instructions:

1. **Activate the Yeast:**
   - In a small bowl, dissolve the yeast in the warm water. Let it sit for about 5-10 minutes, or until it becomes frothy. If using honey or sugar, add it to the water with the yeast.
2. **Prepare the Dough:**
   - In a large mixing bowl, combine the flour and salt.

- Make a well in the center and add the yeast mixture and olive oil or melted butter.
- Mix until a dough starts to form. If the dough is too sticky, add a bit more flour. If it's too dry, add a bit more water.
3. **Knead the Dough:**
   - Turn the dough out onto a floured surface and knead for about 10 minutes, or until the dough is smooth and elastic.
4. **First Rise:**
   - Place the dough in a lightly oiled bowl, cover with plastic wrap or a damp cloth, and let it rise in a warm place for about 1-2 hours, or until it has doubled in size.
5. **Shape the Dough:**
   - Turn the dough out onto a floured surface and divide it into 8-10 equal pieces (for larger pieces, divide less).
   - Flatten each piece into a rectangle and place a few pieces of chocolate (or chocolate chips) in the center.
   - Fold the dough over the chocolate and seal the edges. Shape into a loaf or place the filled pieces in a greased pan or on a parchment-lined baking sheet.
6. **Second Rise:**
   - Cover the dough with a cloth and let it rise for about 30-60 minutes, or until it has puffed up.
7. **Preheat the Oven:**
   - Preheat your oven to 220°C (425°F).
8. **Bake:**
   - Bake in the preheated oven for 15-20 minutes, or until the bread is golden brown and the chocolate is melted.
9. **Cool:**
   - Allow the bread to cool on a wire rack before serving. This helps the chocolate set slightly and prevents it from being too gooey.

Tips:

- **Chocolate:** Use high-quality chocolate for the best flavor. You can use chocolate chips or chopped chocolate.
- **Filling:** For a richer filling, you can add a bit of cocoa powder or a sprinkle of sea salt over the chocolate before sealing the dough.
- **Storage:** Store the bread in an airtight container or plastic bag at room temperature for up to 3 days. It can also be frozen for longer storage.

Pain au Chocolat is a delightful, indulgent treat that pairs perfectly with a cup of coffee or tea. Enjoy the delicious combination of soft bread and melted chocolate!

Pain au Yaourt (Yogurt Bread)

Ingredients:

- **500g (4 cups) all-purpose or bread flour**

- 300g (1.25 cups) plain yogurt (full-fat or low-fat)
- 7g (2 tsp) active dry yeast or instant yeast
- 10g (2 tsp) salt
- 30ml (2 tbsp) olive oil or melted butter
- 1 tablespoon honey or sugar (optional, for a slightly sweeter bread)
- 1 large egg (optional, for egg wash)
- Optional: 1 tablespoon dried herbs or seeds (like sesame or poppy seeds) for added flavor

Instructions:

1. **Activate the Yeast:**
   - In a small bowl, dissolve the yeast in a small amount of warm water (about 50ml or 3 tbsp) if using active dry yeast. Let it sit for about 5-10 minutes, or until it becomes frothy. If using instant yeast, you can skip this step and mix it directly with the flour.
2. **Prepare the Dough:**
   - In a large mixing bowl, combine the flour and salt.
   - Make a well in the center and add the yogurt, yeast mixture (if using active dry yeast), and olive oil or melted butter.
   - Mix until a dough starts to form. If the dough is too sticky, add a bit more flour. If it's too dry, add a bit more yogurt or water.
3. **Knead the Dough:**
   - Turn the dough out onto a floured surface and knead for about 10 minutes, or until the dough is smooth and elastic.
4. **First Rise:**
   - Place the dough in a lightly oiled bowl, cover with plastic wrap or a damp cloth, and let it rise in a warm place for about 1-2 hours, or until it has doubled in size.
5. **Shape the Dough:**
   - Turn the dough out onto a floured surface and shape it into a loaf or divide it into smaller pieces for rolls.
   - Place the shaped dough onto a parchment-lined baking sheet or into a greased loaf pan.
6. **Second Rise:**
   - Cover the dough with a cloth and let it rise for about 30-60 minutes, or until it has puffed up and is nearly doubled in size.
7. **Preheat the Oven:**
   - Preheat your oven to 220°C (425°F).
8. **Optional: Egg Wash:**
   - For a golden, shiny crust, mix 1 egg with a tablespoon of water and brush it over the top of the dough before baking.
9. **Bake:**
   - Bake in the preheated oven for 25-30 minutes, or until the crust is golden brown and the loaf sounds hollow when tapped on the bottom.

10. **Cool:**
    - Allow the bread to cool on a wire rack before slicing. This helps the crumb set and enhances the flavor.

Tips:

- **Yogurt:** Use plain yogurt for the best results. Greek yogurt can be used, but you might need to adjust the amount of flour as it is thicker.
- **Flavor Variations:** You can add dried herbs, seeds, or spices to the dough for added flavor. A sprinkle of sea salt or herbs on top before baking can also enhance the taste.
- **Storage:** Store the bread in an airtight container or plastic bag at room temperature for up to 3 days. It can also be frozen for longer storage.

Pain au Yaourt is a versatile and delicious bread with a lovely texture and subtle tang from the yogurt. Enjoy it fresh from the oven or toasted with your favorite toppings!

Pain au Vin Rouge (Red Wine Bread)

Ingredients:

- **500g (4 cups) all-purpose or bread flour**
- **200ml (0.85 cups) red wine (choose a wine you enjoy drinking)**
- **100ml (0.4 cups) warm water (about 40°C/105°F)**
- **7g (2 tsp) active dry yeast or instant yeast**
- **10g (2 tsp) salt**
- **30ml (2 tbsp) olive oil or melted butter**
- **1 tablespoon honey or sugar (optional, for a slightly sweeter bread)**
- **Optional: 1-2 tablespoons dried herbs (such as rosemary or thyme) or seeds (such as sesame or poppy) for added flavor**

Instructions:

1. **Activate the Yeast:**
    - In a small bowl, dissolve the yeast in the warm water. Let it sit for about 5-10 minutes, or until it becomes frothy. If using honey or sugar, add it to the water with the yeast.
2. **Prepare the Dough:**
    - In a large mixing bowl, combine the flour and salt.
    - Make a well in the center and add the yeast mixture, red wine, and olive oil or melted butter.
    - Mix until a dough starts to form. If the dough is too sticky, add a bit more flour. If it's too dry, add a bit more red wine or water.
3. **Knead the Dough:**
    - Turn the dough out onto a floured surface and knead for about 10 minutes, or until the dough is smooth and elastic.

4. **First Rise:**
   - Place the dough in a lightly oiled bowl, cover with plastic wrap or a damp cloth, and let it rise in a warm place for about 1-2 hours, or until it has doubled in size.
5. **Shape the Dough:**
   - Turn the dough out onto a floured surface and shape it into a loaf or divide it into smaller pieces for rolls.
   - Place the shaped dough onto a parchment-lined baking sheet or into a greased loaf pan.
6. **Second Rise:**
   - Cover the dough with a cloth and let it rise for about 30-60 minutes, or until it has puffed up and is nearly doubled in size.
7. **Preheat the Oven:**
   - Preheat your oven to 220°C (425°F).
8. **Optional: Top the Bread:**
   - If desired, you can sprinkle the top of the dough with dried herbs or seeds before baking.
9. **Bake:**
   - Bake in the preheated oven for 25-30 minutes, or until the crust is golden brown and the loaf sounds hollow when tapped on the bottom.
10. **Cool:**
    - Allow the bread to cool on a wire rack before slicing. This helps the crumb set and enhances the flavor.

Tips:

- **Wine:** Use a good-quality red wine that you enjoy drinking, as its flavor will come through in the bread. A bold red wine like Cabernet Sauvignon or Merlot works well.
- **Flavor Variations:** Adding dried herbs or seeds can enhance the flavor of the bread. Experiment with your favorite combinations.
- **Storage:** Store the bread in an airtight container or plastic bag at room temperature for up to 3 days. It can also be frozen for longer storage.

Pain au Vin Rouge is a unique and flavorful bread that pairs well with cheese, charcuterie, or as an accompaniment to hearty soups and stews. Enjoy the complex flavors and lovely color of this homemade red wine bread!

Pain de Campagne aux Épices (Spiced Country Bread)

Ingredients:

- **500g (4 cups) all-purpose or bread flour**
- **300ml (1.25 cups) warm water (about 40°C/105°F)**
- **7g (2 tsp) active dry yeast or instant yeast**
- **10g (2 tsp) salt**
- **30ml (2 tbsp) olive oil or melted butter**

- **1 tablespoon honey or sugar (optional, for a slightly sweeter dough)**
- **1 tablespoon ground cinnamon**
- **1 teaspoon ground nutmeg**
- **1 teaspoon ground cloves**
- **1 teaspoon ground ginger**
- **Optional: 1 tablespoon dried herbs (such as thyme or rosemary) for added flavor**

Instructions:

1. **Activate the Yeast:**
   - In a small bowl, dissolve the yeast in the warm water. Let it sit for about 5-10 minutes, or until it becomes frothy. If using honey or sugar, add it to the water with the yeast.
2. **Prepare the Dough:**
   - In a large mixing bowl, combine the flour, salt, cinnamon, nutmeg, cloves, and ginger.
   - Make a well in the center and add the yeast mixture and olive oil or melted butter.
   - Mix until a dough starts to form. If the dough is too sticky, add a bit more flour. If it's too dry, add a bit more water.
3. **Knead the Dough:**
   - Turn the dough out onto a floured surface and knead for about 10 minutes, or until the dough is smooth and elastic.
4. **First Rise:**
   - Place the dough in a lightly oiled bowl, cover with plastic wrap or a damp cloth, and let it rise in a warm place for about 1-2 hours, or until it has doubled in size.
5. **Shape the Dough:**
   - Turn the dough out onto a floured surface and shape it into a loaf or divide it into smaller pieces for rolls.
   - Place the shaped dough onto a parchment-lined baking sheet or into a greased loaf pan.
6. **Second Rise:**
   - Cover the dough with a cloth and let it rise for about 30-60 minutes, or until it has puffed up and is nearly doubled in size.
7. **Preheat the Oven:**
   - Preheat your oven to 220°C (425°F).
8. **Bake:**
   - Bake in the preheated oven for 25-30 minutes, or until the crust is golden brown and the loaf sounds hollow when tapped on the bottom.
9. **Cool:**
   - Allow the bread to cool on a wire rack before slicing. This helps the crumb set and enhances the flavor.

Tips:

- **Spices:** Adjust the spice quantities according to your taste preference. You can also experiment with other spices like cardamom or allspice.
- **Flavor Variations:** Adding dried herbs or seeds can complement the spices and add extra flavor.
- **Storage:** Store the bread in an airtight container or plastic bag at room temperature for up to 3 days. It can also be frozen for longer storage.

Pain de Campagne aux Épices offers a comforting and aromatic twist on traditional country bread, making it a perfect addition to any meal or as a standalone treat. Enjoy the blend of spices and rustic texture of this homemade bread!

Pain au Poivre (Pepper Bread)

Ingredients:

- 500g (4 cups) all-purpose or bread flour
- 300ml (1.25 cups) warm water (about 40°C/105°F)
- 7g (2 tsp) active dry yeast or instant yeast
- 10g (2 tsp) salt
- 30ml (2 tbsp) olive oil or melted butter
- 1 tablespoon honey or sugar (optional, for a slightly sweeter dough)
- 2-3 tablespoons freshly ground black pepper (adjust to taste)
- Optional: 1 teaspoon coarsely crushed black pepper for topping

Instructions:

1. **Activate the Yeast:**
   - In a small bowl, dissolve the yeast in the warm water. Let it sit for about 5-10 minutes, or until it becomes frothy. If using honey or sugar, add it to the water with the yeast.
2. **Prepare the Dough:**
   - In a large mixing bowl, combine the flour, salt, and freshly ground black pepper.
   - Make a well in the center and add the yeast mixture and olive oil or melted butter.
   - Mix until a dough starts to form. If the dough is too sticky, add a bit more flour. If it's too dry, add a bit more water.
3. **Knead the Dough:**
   - Turn the dough out onto a floured surface and knead for about 10 minutes, or until the dough is smooth and elastic.
4. **First Rise:**
   - Place the dough in a lightly oiled bowl, cover with plastic wrap or a damp cloth, and let it rise in a warm place for about 1-2 hours, or until it has doubled in size.
5. **Shape the Dough:**
   - Turn the dough out onto a floured surface and shape it into a loaf or divide it into smaller pieces for rolls.

- Place the shaped dough onto a parchment-lined baking sheet or into a greased loaf pan.
- If desired, sprinkle coarsely crushed black pepper on top of the dough for extra flavor and visual appeal.

6. **Second Rise:**
   - Cover the dough with a cloth and let it rise for about 30-60 minutes, or until it has puffed up and is nearly doubled in size.
7. **Preheat the Oven:**
   - Preheat your oven to 220°C (425°F).
8. **Bake:**
   - Bake in the preheated oven for 25-30 minutes, or until the crust is golden brown and the loaf sounds hollow when tapped on the bottom.
9. **Cool:**
   - Allow the bread to cool on a wire rack before slicing. This helps the crumb set and enhances the flavor.

Tips:

- **Pepper:** Use freshly ground black pepper for the best flavor. You can adjust the amount of pepper based on your heat tolerance and flavor preference.
- **Flavor Variations:** Experiment with other types of pepper, such as white or green pepper, for different flavor profiles.
- **Storage:** Store the bread in an airtight container or plastic bag at room temperature for up to 3 days. It can also be frozen for longer storage.

Pain au Poivre offers a delightful peppery twist on traditional bread, adding a bit of spice and complexity. It pairs wonderfully with cheeses, cured meats, or simply as a flavorful accompaniment to any meal. Enjoy the robust flavor and aroma of this homemade bread!

Pain à la Moutarde (Mustard Bread)

Ingredients:

- **500g (4 cups) all-purpose or bread flour**
- **300ml (1.25 cups) warm water (about 40°C/105°F)**
- **7g (2 tsp) active dry yeast or instant yeast**
- **10g (2 tsp) salt**
- **30ml (2 tbsp) olive oil or melted butter**
- **2-3 tablespoons Dijon mustard or your favorite mustard (adjust to taste)**
- **1 tablespoon honey or sugar (optional, for a slightly sweeter bread)**
- **Optional: 1 tablespoon mustard seeds for added texture**

Instructions:

1. **Activate the Yeast:**

- In a small bowl, dissolve the yeast in the warm water. Let it sit for about 5-10 minutes, or until it becomes frothy. If using honey or sugar, add it to the water with the yeast.
2. **Prepare the Dough:**
   - In a large mixing bowl, combine the flour and salt.
   - Make a well in the center and add the yeast mixture, olive oil or melted butter, and Dijon mustard.
   - Mix until a dough starts to form. If the dough is too sticky, add a bit more flour. If it's too dry, add a bit more water.
3. **Knead the Dough:**
   - Turn the dough out onto a floured surface and knead for about 10 minutes, or until the dough is smooth and elastic. If using mustard seeds, gently fold them into the dough during kneading.
4. **First Rise:**
   - Place the dough in a lightly oiled bowl, cover with plastic wrap or a damp cloth, and let it rise in a warm place for about 1-2 hours, or until it has doubled in size.
5. **Shape the Dough:**
   - Turn the dough out onto a floured surface and shape it into a loaf or divide it into smaller pieces for rolls.
   - Place the shaped dough onto a parchment-lined baking sheet or into a greased loaf pan.
6. **Second Rise:**
   - Cover the dough with a cloth and let it rise for about 30-60 minutes, or until it has puffed up and is nearly doubled in size.
7. **Preheat the Oven:**
   - Preheat your oven to 220°C (425°F).
8. **Bake:**
   - Bake in the preheated oven for 25-30 minutes, or until the crust is golden brown and the loaf sounds hollow when tapped on the bottom.
9. **Cool:**
   - Allow the bread to cool on a wire rack before slicing. This helps the crumb set and enhances the flavor.

Tips:

- **Mustard:** Adjust the amount of mustard based on your taste preference. If you prefer a milder flavor, use less mustard.
- **Mustard Seeds:** Adding mustard seeds can give an extra burst of flavor and texture. You can also use them as a topping before baking.
- **Flavor Variations:** For added depth of flavor, you can incorporate herbs or spices, such as thyme or paprika, into the dough.
- **Storage:** Store the bread in an airtight container or plastic bag at room temperature for up to 3 days. It can also be frozen for longer storage.

Pain à la Moutarde is a savory and aromatic bread that brings a unique twist to traditional bread recipes. Its tangy mustard flavor pairs well with a variety of dishes, making it a versatile and delightful addition to your baking repertoire. Enjoy!

Pain au Chèvre (Goat Cheese Bread)

Ingredients:

- **500g (4 cups) all-purpose or bread flour**
- **300ml (1.25 cups) warm water (about 40°C/105°F)**
- **7g (2 tsp) active dry yeast or instant yeast**
- **10g (2 tsp) salt**
- **30ml (2 tbsp) olive oil or melted butter**
- **150g (5.3 oz) goat cheese, crumbled**
- **1 tablespoon honey or sugar (optional, for a slightly sweeter dough)**
- **Optional: 1 tablespoon dried herbs (such as thyme, rosemary, or oregano) or freshly ground black pepper for added flavor**

Instructions:

1. **Activate the Yeast:**
   - In a small bowl, dissolve the yeast in the warm water. Let it sit for about 5-10 minutes, or until it becomes frothy. If using honey or sugar, add it to the water with the yeast.
2. **Prepare the Dough:**
   - In a large mixing bowl, combine the flour and salt.
   - Make a well in the center and add the yeast mixture and olive oil or melted butter.
   - Mix until a dough starts to form. If the dough is too sticky, add a bit more flour. If it's too dry, add a bit more water.
3. **Knead the Dough:**
   - Turn the dough out onto a floured surface and knead for about 10 minutes, or until the dough is smooth and elastic.
   - Gently fold in the crumbled goat cheese during the last few minutes of kneading. If using, also fold in dried herbs or black pepper.
4. **First Rise:**
   - Place the dough in a lightly oiled bowl, cover with plastic wrap or a damp cloth, and let it rise in a warm place for about 1-2 hours, or until it has doubled in size.
5. **Shape the Dough:**
   - Turn the dough out onto a floured surface and shape it into a loaf or divide it into smaller pieces for rolls.
   - Place the shaped dough onto a parchment-lined baking sheet or into a greased loaf pan.
6. **Second Rise:**

- Cover the dough with a cloth and let it rise for about 30-60 minutes, or until it has puffed up and is nearly doubled in size.
7. **Preheat the Oven:**
    - Preheat your oven to 220°C (425°F).
8. **Bake:**
    - Bake in the preheated oven for 25-30 minutes, or until the crust is golden brown and the loaf sounds hollow when tapped on the bottom.
9. **Cool:**
    - Allow the bread to cool on a wire rack before slicing. This helps the crumb set and enhances the flavor.

Tips:

- **Goat Cheese:** Use a high-quality goat cheese for the best flavor. You can also experiment with different varieties, such as herbed goat cheese.
- **Flavor Variations:** Adding herbs or spices can enhance the flavor. Freshly ground black pepper or a sprinkle of sea salt on top before baking can add extra depth.
- **Storage:** Store the bread in an airtight container or plastic bag at room temperature for up to 3 days. It can also be frozen for longer storage.

Pain au Chèvre is a delicious and savory bread that combines the tangy richness of goat cheese with the satisfying texture of homemade bread. It's a wonderful addition to any meal and pairs especially well with salads, charcuterie, or just on its own. Enjoy!

Pain aux Framboises (Raspberry Bread)

Ingredients:

- **500g (4 cups) all-purpose flour**
- **200ml (0.85 cups) warm milk (about 40°C/105°F)**
- **7g (2 tsp) active dry yeast or instant yeast**
- **100g (0.5 cups) granulated sugar**
- **10g (2 tsp) salt**
- **80ml (0.3 cups) melted butter or vegetable oil**
- **1 large egg**
- **150g (1.5 cups) fresh or frozen raspberries**
- **Optional: 1 teaspoon vanilla extract or almond extract for added flavor**
- **Optional: 1 tablespoon flour (to coat the raspberries)**

Instructions:

1. **Activate the Yeast:**
   - In a small bowl, dissolve the yeast in the warm milk. Let it sit for about 5-10 minutes, or until it becomes frothy.
2. **Prepare the Dough:**
   - In a large mixing bowl, combine the flour, sugar, and salt.
   - Make a well in the center and add the yeast mixture, melted butter or oil, and egg. If using, add vanilla or almond extract.
   - Mix until a dough starts to form. If the dough is too sticky, add a bit more flour. If it's too dry, add a bit more milk.
3. **Knead the Dough:**
   - Turn the dough out onto a floured surface and knead for about 10 minutes, or until the dough is smooth and elastic.
4. **Prepare the Raspberries:**
   - If using frozen raspberries, gently toss them with a tablespoon of flour to prevent them from sinking and bleeding too much color into the dough.
5. **Incorporate the Raspberries:**
   - Gently fold the raspberries into the dough during the last few minutes of kneading. Be careful not to crush them too much.
6. **First Rise:**
   - Place the dough in a lightly oiled bowl, cover with plastic wrap or a damp cloth, and let it rise in a warm place for about 1-2 hours, or until it has doubled in size.
7. **Shape the Dough:**
   - Turn the dough out onto a floured surface and shape it into a loaf or divide it into smaller pieces for rolls.
   - Place the shaped dough onto a parchment-lined baking sheet or into a greased loaf pan.
8. **Second Rise:**
   - Cover the dough with a cloth and let it rise for about 30-60 minutes, or until it has puffed up and is nearly doubled in size.

9. **Preheat the Oven:**
   - Preheat your oven to 180°C (350°F).
10. **Bake:**
    - Bake in the preheated oven for 30-35 minutes, or until the crust is golden brown and the loaf sounds hollow when tapped on the bottom.
11. **Cool:**
    - Allow the bread to cool on a wire rack before slicing. This helps the crumb set and enhances the flavor.

Tips:

- **Raspberries:** Fresh raspberries work best, but frozen raspberries can be used. Just be sure to thaw and drain them well before adding them to the dough.
- **Sweetness:** Adjust the sugar based on your preference and the tartness of the raspberries.
- **Storage:** Store the bread in an airtight container or plastic bag at room temperature for up to 3 days. It can also be frozen for longer storage.

Pain aux Framboises offers a delightful mix of sweet and tangy flavors, making it a lovely treat for any occasion. Enjoy the vibrant bursts of raspberry throughout the soft, flavorful bread!

Pain au Basilic (Basil Bread)

Ingredients:

- 500g (4 cups) all-purpose or bread flour
- 300ml (1.25 cups) warm water (about 40°C/105°F)
- 7g (2 tsp) active dry yeast or instant yeast
- 10g (2 tsp) salt
- 30ml (2 tbsp) olive oil
- 1 tablespoon honey or sugar (optional, for a slightly sweeter dough)
- 1/4 cup fresh basil leaves, finely chopped (or 2 tablespoons dried basil)
- Optional: 1 tablespoon chopped garlic or grated Parmesan cheese for added flavor

Instructions:

1. **Activate the Yeast:**
   - In a small bowl, dissolve the yeast in the warm water. Let it sit for about 5-10 minutes, or until it becomes frothy. If using honey or sugar, add it to the water with the yeast.
2. **Prepare the Dough:**
   - In a large mixing bowl, combine the flour and salt.
   - Make a well in the center and add the yeast mixture, olive oil, and finely chopped basil (or dried basil). If using garlic or Parmesan cheese, add them as well.

        - Mix until a dough starts to form. If the dough is too sticky, add a bit more flour. If it's too dry, add a bit more water.
3. **Knead the Dough:**
        - Turn the dough out onto a floured surface and knead for about 10 minutes, or until the dough is smooth and elastic.
4. **First Rise:**
        - Place the dough in a lightly oiled bowl, cover with plastic wrap or a damp cloth, and let it rise in a warm place for about 1-2 hours, or until it has doubled in size.
5. **Shape the Dough:**
        - Turn the dough out onto a floured surface and shape it into a loaf or divide it into smaller pieces for rolls.
        - Place the shaped dough onto a parchment-lined baking sheet or into a greased loaf pan.
6. **Second Rise:**
        - Cover the dough with a cloth and let it rise for about 30-60 minutes, or until it has puffed up and is nearly doubled in size.
7. **Preheat the Oven:**
        - Preheat your oven to 220°C (425°F).
8. **Bake:**
        - Bake in the preheated oven for 25-30 minutes, or until the crust is golden brown and the loaf sounds hollow when tapped on the bottom.
9. **Cool:**
        - Allow the bread to cool on a wire rack before slicing. This helps the crumb set and enhances the flavor.

Tips:

- **Basil:** Use fresh basil for the best flavor, but dried basil can be used as well. If using dried basil, add it along with the flour and salt.
- **Flavor Variations:** You can add additional ingredients like chopped sun-dried tomatoes or olives for a more complex flavor profile.
- **Storage:** Store the bread in an airtight container or plastic bag at room temperature for up to 3 days. It can also be frozen for longer storage.

Pain au Basilic brings a fresh and aromatic touch to your bread basket, making it a delightful addition to any meal. Enjoy the fragrant basil notes and the soft, flavorful crumb of this homemade bread!

Pain au Coing (Quince Bread)

Ingredients:

- **500g (4 cups) all-purpose or bread flour**
- **300ml (1.25 cups) warm water (about 40°C/105°F)**
- **7g (2 tsp) active dry yeast or instant yeast**

- **10g (2 tsp) salt**
- **30ml (2 tbsp) olive oil or melted butter**
- **100g (1/2 cup) quince paste or quince jam (adjust to taste)**
- **1 tablespoon honey or sugar (optional, for a slightly sweeter dough)**
- **1 large egg (for egg wash, optional)**
- **Optional: 1/2 teaspoon ground cinnamon or nutmeg for added warmth**

Instructions:

1. **Activate the Yeast:**
   - In a small bowl, dissolve the yeast in the warm water. Let it sit for about 5-10 minutes, or until it becomes frothy. If using honey or sugar, add it to the water with the yeast.
2. **Prepare the Dough:**
   - In a large mixing bowl, combine the flour and salt. If using, add ground cinnamon or nutmeg.
   - Make a well in the center and add the yeast mixture, olive oil or melted butter, and quince paste or jam.
   - Mix until a dough starts to form. If the dough is too sticky, add a bit more flour. If it's too dry, add a bit more water.
3. **Knead the Dough:**
   - Turn the dough out onto a floured surface and knead for about 10 minutes, or until the dough is smooth and elastic.
4. **First Rise:**
   - Place the dough in a lightly oiled bowl, cover with plastic wrap or a damp cloth, and let it rise in a warm place for about 1-2 hours, or until it has doubled in size.
5. **Shape the Dough:**
   - Turn the dough out onto a floured surface and shape it into a loaf or divide it into smaller pieces for rolls.
   - Place the shaped dough onto a parchment-lined baking sheet or into a greased loaf pan.
6. **Second Rise:**
   - Cover the dough with a cloth and let it rise for about 30-60 minutes, or until it has puffed up and is nearly doubled in size.
7. **Preheat the Oven:**
   - Preheat your oven to 220°C (425°F).
8. **Bake:**
   - If desired, brush the top of the dough with a beaten egg for a golden finish.
   - Bake in the preheated oven for 25-30 minutes, or until the crust is golden brown and the loaf sounds hollow when tapped on the bottom.
9. **Cool:**
   - Allow the bread to cool on a wire rack before slicing. This helps the crumb set and enhances the flavor.

Tips:

- **Quince Paste:** If using quince paste, cut it into small pieces before mixing it into the dough. You can also use quince jam for a more uniform sweetness.
- **Flavor Variations:** Adding spices like cinnamon or nutmeg can complement the quince flavor. Adjust the spices according to your taste.
- **Storage:** Store the bread in an airtight container or plastic bag at room temperature for up to 3 days. It can also be frozen for longer storage.

Pain au Coing offers a unique and flavorful twist on traditional bread, with the fragrant and sweet notes of quince making it a special treat. Enjoy the subtle fruitiness and soft texture of this delightful bread!

Pain à la Pistache (Pistachio Bread)

Ingredients:

- **500g (4 cups) all-purpose or bread flour**
- **300ml (1.25 cups) warm water (about 40°C/105°F)**
- **7g (2 tsp) active dry yeast or instant yeast**
- **10g (2 tsp) salt**
- **30ml (2 tbsp) olive oil or melted butter**
- **100g (0.75 cup) shelled pistachios, chopped**
- **50g (1/4 cup) granulated sugar (optional, for a slightly sweeter bread)**
- **1 tablespoon honey (optional)**
- **1 large egg (for egg wash, optional)**

Instructions:

1. **Activate the Yeast:**
   - In a small bowl, dissolve the yeast in the warm water. Let it sit for about 5-10 minutes, or until it becomes frothy. If using sugar or honey, add it to the water with the yeast.
2. **Prepare the Dough:**
   - In a large mixing bowl, combine the flour and salt.
   - Make a well in the center and add the yeast mixture, olive oil or melted butter.
   - Mix until a dough starts to form. If the dough is too sticky, add a bit more flour. If it's too dry, add a bit more water.
3. **Incorporate the Pistachios:**
   - Turn the dough out onto a floured surface and knead for about 10 minutes, or until smooth and elastic. During the last few minutes of kneading, gently fold in the chopped pistachios.
4. **First Rise:**
   - Place the dough in a lightly oiled bowl, cover with plastic wrap or a damp cloth, and let it rise in a warm place for about 1-2 hours, or until it has doubled in size.
5. **Shape the Dough:**
   - Turn the dough out onto a floured surface and shape it into a loaf or divide it into smaller pieces for rolls.
   - Place the shaped dough onto a parchment-lined baking sheet or into a greased loaf pan.
6. **Second Rise:**
   - Cover the dough with a cloth and let it rise for about 30-60 minutes, or until it has puffed up and is nearly doubled in size.
7. **Preheat the Oven:**
   - Preheat your oven to 220°C (425°F).
8. **Bake:**
   - If desired, brush the top of the dough with a beaten egg for a glossy finish.
   - Bake in the preheated oven for 25-30 minutes, or until the crust is golden brown and the loaf sounds hollow when tapped on the bottom.

9. **Cool:**
    - Allow the bread to cool on a wire rack before slicing to set the crumb and enhance flavor.

Tips:

- **Pistachios:** Use shelled pistachios and chop them coarsely for better distribution throughout the bread. You can toast them lightly for extra flavor if desired.
- **Sweetness:** Adjust the amount of sugar and honey based on your taste preference.
- **Storage:** Store the bread in an airtight container or plastic bag at room temperature for up to 3 days. It can also be frozen for longer storage.

Pain à la Pistache is a flavorful and unique bread that combines the rich, buttery taste of pistachios with the comforting texture of homemade bread. Enjoy this special treat as part of any meal or on its own!

Pain au Cacao et Orange (Chocolate Orange Bread)

Ingredients:

- 500g (4 cups) all-purpose or bread flour
- 300ml (1.25 cups) warm milk (about 40°C/105°F)
- 7g (2 tsp) active dry yeast or instant yeast
- 100g (1/2 cup) granulated sugar
- 10g (2 tsp) salt
- 30ml (2 tbsp) unsalted butter, melted
- 1 large egg
- 50g (1/3 cup) unsweetened cocoa powder
- 100g (3.5 oz) semi-sweet chocolate chips or chopped chocolate
- Zest of 1 large orange
- Juice of 1/2 large orange (about 60ml)
- Optional: 1 teaspoon vanilla extract or orange extract for added flavor

Instructions:

1. **Activate the Yeast:**
    - In a small bowl, dissolve the yeast in the warm milk. Let it sit for about 5-10 minutes, or until it becomes frothy.
2. **Prepare the Dough:**
    - In a large mixing bowl, combine the flour, sugar, cocoa powder, and salt.
    - Make a well in the center and add the yeast mixture, melted butter, egg, orange zest, and orange juice. If using, add vanilla or orange extract.
    - Mix until a dough starts to form. If the dough is too sticky, add a bit more flour. If it's too dry, add a bit more milk.
3. **Knead the Dough:**

- Turn the dough out onto a floured surface and knead for about 10 minutes, or until smooth and elastic.
- During the last few minutes of kneading, gently fold in the chocolate chips or chopped chocolate.

4. **First Rise:**
   - Place the dough in a lightly oiled bowl, cover with plastic wrap or a damp cloth, and let it rise in a warm place for about 1-2 hours, or until it has doubled in size.
5. **Shape the Dough:**
   - Turn the dough out onto a floured surface and shape it into a loaf or divide it into smaller pieces for rolls.
   - Place the shaped dough onto a parchment-lined baking sheet or into a greased loaf pan.
6. **Second Rise:**
   - Cover the dough with a cloth and let it rise for about 30-60 minutes, or until it has puffed up and is nearly doubled in size.
7. **Preheat the Oven:**
   - Preheat your oven to 180°C (350°F).
8. **Bake:**
   - Bake in the preheated oven for 30-35 minutes, or until the crust is firm and the loaf sounds hollow when tapped on the bottom.
9. **Cool:**
   - Allow the bread to cool on a wire rack before slicing. This helps the crumb set and enhances the flavor.

Tips:

- **Chocolate:** Use high-quality semi-sweet chocolate for the best flavor. You can also use dark chocolate for a richer taste.
- **Orange Zest and Juice:** Fresh orange zest and juice will give the bread a bright, natural flavor. Avoid using bottled orange juice if possible.
- **Storage:** Store the bread in an airtight container or plastic bag at room temperature for up to 3 days. It can also be frozen for longer storage.

Pain au Cacao et Orange offers a delightful blend of chocolate and citrus flavors, making it a wonderful addition to any meal or as a special treat. Enjoy the rich, aromatic taste of this homemade bread!

Pain d'Échalote (Shallot Bread)

Ingredients:

- **500g (4 cups) all-purpose or bread flour**
- **300ml (1.25 cups) warm water (about 40°C/105°F)**
- **7g (2 tsp) active dry yeast or instant yeast**
- **10g (2 tsp) salt**

- **30ml (2 tbsp) olive oil or melted butter**
- **4-5 small shallots, finely chopped**
- **1 tablespoon honey or sugar (optional, for a slightly sweeter dough)**
- **1 large egg (for egg wash, optional)**
- **Optional: 1 tablespoon fresh thyme or rosemary for additional flavor**

Instructions:

1. **Prepare the Shallots:**
   - Heat a small amount of olive oil in a pan over medium heat. Add the finely chopped shallots and sauté until they are soft and translucent, about 5-7 minutes. Allow them to cool slightly.
2. **Activate the Yeast:**
   - In a small bowl, dissolve the yeast in the warm water. Let it sit for about 5-10 minutes, or until it becomes frothy. If using honey or sugar, add it to the water with the yeast.
3. **Prepare the Dough:**
   - In a large mixing bowl, combine the flour and salt. If using, add thyme or rosemary.
   - Make a well in the center and add the yeast mixture, olive oil or melted butter, and sautéed shallots.
   - Mix until a dough starts to form. If the dough is too sticky, add a bit more flour. If it's too dry, add a bit more water.
4. **Knead the Dough:**
   - Turn the dough out onto a floured surface and knead for about 10 minutes, or until smooth and elastic.
5. **First Rise:**
   - Place the dough in a lightly oiled bowl, cover with plastic wrap or a damp cloth, and let it rise in a warm place for about 1-2 hours, or until it has doubled in size.
6. **Shape the Dough:**
   - Turn the dough out onto a floured surface and shape it into a loaf or divide it into smaller pieces for rolls.
   - Place the shaped dough onto a parchment-lined baking sheet or into a greased loaf pan.
7. **Second Rise:**
   - Cover the dough with a cloth and let it rise for about 30-60 minutes, or until it has puffed up and is nearly doubled in size.
8. **Preheat the Oven:**
   - Preheat your oven to 220°C (425°F).
9. **Bake:**
   - If desired, brush the top of the dough with a beaten egg for a glossy finish.
   - Bake in the preheated oven for 25-30 minutes, or until the crust is golden brown and the loaf sounds hollow when tapped on the bottom.
10. **Cool:**

- Allow the bread to cool on a wire rack before slicing to set the crumb and enhance flavor.

Tips:

- **Shallots:** Ensure the shallots are well-cooked and cooled before adding them to the dough to prevent them from affecting the dough's consistency.
- **Herbs:** Fresh herbs like thyme or rosemary can complement the shallots nicely, but are optional.
- **Storage:** Store the bread in an airtight container or plastic bag at room temperature for up to 3 days. It can also be frozen for longer storage.

Pain d'Échalote offers a savory twist on traditional bread, enriched with the delicate sweetness of shallots. Enjoy it fresh out of the oven or toasted with your favorite spreads!